To Reuben

Grace Foakes

My Part of the River

Futura Publications Limited
A Futura Book

A Futura Book

First published in two volumes in 1972 and 1974
by Shepheard-Walwyn (Publishers) Limited
entitled BETWEEN HIGH WALLS and MY PART
OF THE RIVER
First Futura Publications edition 1976

ISBN 0 8600 7350 5
Printed in Great Britain by
Hazell Watson & Viney Ltd
Aylesbury, Bucks

Futura Publications Limited
110 Warner Road,
Camberwell, London SE5

BETWEEN HIGH WALLS
A London Childhood

INTRODUCTION

This book is indeed an historical gem, which glows with a different aspect of deeply moving truth from every one of its small and finely cut facets.

That it is the work of a woman who has chosen to give an honest account of her life, not withholding any blemishes in those whom she loved, or exaggerating her own virtues, nor asking for compassion by sentimentalising her woes, makes this slender volume something much more than a tale; it is a revelation and a salutary lesson in heroism. Written in an uninhibited style, her statements grip the reader by their very simplicity, making us share her hard, yet happy life, and introducing a great many to a way of life and living conditions that they can scarcely credit to have existed.

Her description of the locality, much of which was destroyed during the 1939–45 war, are faithfully penned, for its grim brickwork cast its shadows over her consciousness just as it limited her visual horizons; but where the sun penetrated she saw beauty. We learn of social problems from the sufferer's angle, even as we are honoured by being allowed to share in the glorious happiness of the family's Christmas dinner.

Personally, I am so moved by this book because I have worked and lived in the area of Stepney, which includes Wapping, Shadwell and St. George-in-the-East, for the greater part of my life, and know that the living conditions described are not exaggerated. Neither is the poverty.

We are shown how an upright way of life was possible in spite of the constant battle to keep body and soul alive; and how, despite the fact that the family were not 'Church-goers' (as distinct from sending the children to Sunday school), the ethical and spiritual sides of life were successfully inculcated into the children by their parents.

That Mrs Foakes should have given to the world of today this chronicle of her life in an era beyond the ken of the rising generations, is a most fortunate event, whilst to the few older generations like myself who still survive, it brings back memories that are full of admiration for those thousands of men and women who had to rear their families without any 'mod. cons' – and made so good a job of it.

Stepney, July 1972   *Rose Henriques*

PROLOGUE

If you had been a visitor to London when I was a child, Tower Bridge would have been one of the first places of interest you would have gone to see. It was a beautiful bridge, spanning the Thames. From the north side you could look across and see the Tower of London. If you looked over the side of the bridge, you saw all kinds of river craft. There were tugs, barges, police boats, and large ocean-going ships. When an extra large vessel, too tall to pass underneath, needed to pass further up river the bridge would be opened. A bell was rung and all traffic was stopped at either end. The bridge would open up from the centre until it stood upright, with half on each side. The ship could then pass through and proceed to whatever wharf or warehouse it was destined for. The halves of the bridge were then lowered and the traffic allowed to resume its journeyings.

You would have seen large docks, wharves and warehouses, where ships from far away places were berthed. Great cranes would load and unload cargo of every kind. Here men would earn their living. It was a magnificent sight, and visitors would stand and gaze at the busy scene and think how wonderful it all was.

But I want to take you for another visit to show you what lay on the other side of these wharves and warehouses.

As you approached Tower Bridge from the City side you came to some stone steps, which led down to the entrance to the warehouses and to St. Katherine's Way. This was a narrow road with high walls on either side. At intervals, between each warehouse, there was a short dark passage, just wide enough for a man to walk through, leading to the river. These were known as 'Shoreways'. Walls! Nothing but high walls until you came to St. Katherine's Bridge, a dock bridge, which at

9

times would open to let shipping pass from the Thames into London Docks. On you walked with the high brick walls on either side. They must have been more than sixty feet high. If you wanted to see the sky you had to stand and look straight up – you were closed in on every side – and if you were a small child it could be very frightening should you chance to walk there at night.

Walking on still further you came to another dock bridge, Hermitage Bridge. It did not open, but formed part of the dock basin. On crossing this bridge the scene changed. Now there were warehouses on one side only, the river side. Opposite them was a large block of tenement flats, which boasted the name 'Royal Jubilee Buildings'. I believe they were built during the Royal Jubilee Year of Queen Victoria. Nothing less royal you ever saw! Iron railings enclosed them at the front and a great cobblestone yard lay stretched behind its whole length. The tenants used it for drying washing. Behind and around these tenement buildings were narrow, mean little streets and alleyways, with small drab houses, mostly with underground kitchens, where people lived in semi-darkness for most of their lives. Three or four families occupied one house, sharing the kitchen with its one cold water tap. Sometimes the tap was in the yard outside.

This was not the world as it is today. Hot water systems were unheard of, lighting was by gas or paraffin lamps and there was no electricity. Yet the people who lived there took great pride in their homes. They were mostly dockers with large families and small incomes. This was a little community which lived almost entirely within itself. You knew everyone else and everyone else knew you.

In these surroundings I spent my childhood. I can see it all so clearly in my mind that I feel compelled to write down as many things as I can remember. There must be many older people who will recall those days and places. As I grow older I shall forget, as older people do, but I shall open my book and it will all come to life again.

CHAPTER ONE

WAPPING

We lived in Wapping High Street. Now 'High Street' today usually means a street where there are shops of all kinds, but our High Street had very few shops. It stretched from one end of Wapping to the other, with the dock bridges in between. On each side were wharves and warehouses. The roads were made of cobblestones, with a narrow path on one side only. All traffic was pulled by horses for there were no motor cars. The drivers of these horses had great whips, with which they beat them to encourage them to pull faster. Sometimes two horses would be harnessed to one cart if the load was heavy. In winter the roads would be in a very slippery state and sometimes the poor creatures would stumble and fall. Then the driver would dismount and whip them until they struggled to their feet again. This was very cruel, for in most cases the load was far too heavy. My sister and I would watch while this went on. It was an everyday sight and nobody seemed to care, but we would hold hands and cry in sympathy for the poor creatures.

In these days of clean air and smokeless fuel, it is hard to imagine what a London fog was like sixty years ago. Everyone had a coal fire, factories sent out great clouds of sooty grime, ships and tugs were driven by steam, their funnels belching out great quantities of thick black smoke. Winter would bring to the river such fogs as you do not see today. The air was so thick and yellow that you could not see where you were going. To avoid losing yourself, you had to run your hand along the walls as you walked.

They made everything dirty. Big black pieces of soot would settle everywhere. All day the ships would send out their mournful fog warning, for it was very dangerous on the river when a fog descended. Shipping was at an almost total stand-still and those boats which continued on their way were in constant danger of collision. Many men fell overboard during these fogs and, since it was impossible to find them in these conditions, they were drowned. These fogs could last for many days. They were 'killer fogs' (we called them 'pea-soupers') and sometimes those who had a weak chest found it impossible to breathe. Many elderly people and young babies died as a result of being out in one of these fogs.

Great was our relief when the sun eventually shone, dispersing the gloom, and bringing things back to normal again.

CHAPTER TWO

WHERE I SPENT MY CHILDHOOD

When I was a little girl I lived with my parents, my three brothers and my sister in one of the tenement flats in Royal Jubilee Buildings. It consisted of two bedrooms and a kitchen. My parents occupied one bedroom, and we five children shared the other. Mother divided the room with a large clothes-horse covered with a sheet, to separate boys from girls. All the available space was taken up by three beds and my father's large toolchest. The walls were distempered in a dull brown colour. What a dark and cheerless room it was.

My parents' bedroom contained a double bed, a chest of drawers, a table and a chair, two boxes placed one on top of the other, and a small marble wash-stand. There was also a sewing machine. The kitchen, which served as the main room, had four Windsor chairs, my father's chair, two stools, and a kitchen table with two leaves which we opened or shut as required. At one end of the room was a small window, in front of which stood a large clothes-wringer with wooden rollers. This shut out much of the light and took up nearly all the space at that end of the room. In one corner was a black tin sink, six inches deep, and over it a cold water tap. Next to this was a black iron gas cooker, and then the fireplace. This was an open affair with a flat top which was open at the back to allow the smoke to go up. An oven was attached to the side of the grate – it heated when you lit the fire. There was no control on this; you simply guessed the heat and cooked accordingly.

It was surprising what could be cooked in this oven, once you got the hang of it. My mother had a baking tin, which had a division in the centre. In one side she would put potatoes for baking, in the other Yorkshire pudding. Then she would put a meat stand in and on top of this went the joint. The meat, the potatoes and the Yorkshire pudding all cooked together, and the tin was turned round every now and then so that each side had a chance to be next to the hot dividing wall between the fire and the oven. Into an iron saucepan on top of the open fire would go whatever vegetable was to be cooked. When it boiled it was drawn back just enough to keep it simmering. A large iron kettle was always heating on the other side of the fire, so that there was hot water whenever it was required. These cooking utensils would get very dirty and sooty, and sometimes if it was windy or the chimney wanted sweeping smoke would blow down, giving everything a smokey taste. The ashes and cinders from the fire would fall into the hearth below, and would make such a mess on everything. It was continually being cleaned up. My mother had an iron contraption which she called 'the Tidy'. She placed it on the hearth in front of the fire in an effort to trap the ashes as they fell, for the hearth was cleaned each morning with hearthstone to make it look white. On the hearth stood a steel fender which too was cleaned each day, with emery paper. This all looked very nice until you lit the fire. The fire was nice too, but not so the mess. There was dust everywhere.

On the other side of the hearth and about two feet from the floor was the cupboard in which everything had to be kept, since there was no storage space anywhere else. Underneath

the cupboard and hidden from view by a small curtain were all
the boots, and the cat box.

This then was the kitchen where seven people ate, played and
worked. But it was warm and it was home. It was the place
where my mother could always be found – and that was all that
mattered.

CHAPTER THREE

MY FATHER

I found my father a very hard man to understand when I was
young. He was very short and thin and had large blue eyes. I
could have loved him as I did my mother, but he seemed to
hold us off so that we could not approach him or sit on his knee
as children love to do. I believe he had a hard life as a child,
and I know that he left school at the age of ten and started
work. This may have had something to do with it, but I can
only surmise. In later life I came to love him very much, but at
the time I speak of he was an unsociable man, unfriendly even
towards the people closest to him. My mother could never have
a neighbour in for a cup of tea or a chat, and we could not ask
our friends in either. He did not drink or smoke and had no
kind of hobby. I never knew him to have a close friend as the
other men did.

Everything he did had to be precise. If he chopped the sticks
for the fire, each stick would be the same length and thickness
as all the others, and they would all be stacked on a ledge with
not one out of place. The floor was covered with mock lino (we
had no carpets) and if a portion wore out he would carefully
cut it away and measure for another piece to be fitted in.
Always it fitted perfectly. His motto was 'If a thing is worth
doing, it is worth doing well'. He would not borrow or lend nor
allow my mother to do so. In our household his word was law
and nobody dared dispute it.

He worked hard when in a job and saw to it that we children learned the meaning of work. My mother did not have much pleasure but I do not remember her ever complaining – except on Sunday afternoons when Father would undress and get into bed, leaving her to mend his working clothes while he had his rest. This she resented very much, for the clothes were dirty from the work he had been doing and she hated handling anything that was not clean.

We had a sewing machine of the treadle type which my father had decided I must learn to use. He would make me sit at that machine and, after showing me how to thread the boat-shaped bobbin and to fix the top cotton, he would stand over me and I would have to practise on it. If the wheel went backwards instead of forwards the cotton would break, so he gave me lessons on starting it so that the wheel always moved the right way. When I had mastered this he would then give me an old piece of material and would stand and watch while I practised doing 'straight lines'. This I simply could not do while he watched me, but he would not let me give up. Eventually I mastered this too and was able to machine perfectly. I have never forgotten those lessons or his rare smile of pleasure when he told me 'I knew you could do it'. I still have an old treadle machine and would not part with it for all the modern ones. Each time I use it, the words still come to my mind 'I knew you could do it'.

I do not know how old I was when this little event happened but I recall it clearly. We woke up one morning and Father told me to go and call a neighbour who lived several streets away. I was to say she was wanted quickly as Mother was not well. She came about an hour afterwards. Then suddenly we children heard a baby's cry and we knew we had another brother or sister. When she left a little later the neighbour told my father she would not come again as Gracie was now becoming a big girl and could carry on without her. In those days you had no midwife. Neighbours looked after each other. The doctor usually came only at the time of the delivery as each visit had to be paid for and people just could not afford more than one. Therefore the arrangement was made with whoever you were most friendly with.

This particular time was unfortunate for me. I remember it was a Sunday and we were sent to Sunday School as usual. On arriving home I found Father had heated the copper and had the tin bath arranged on two chairs, just at the right height to fit my small figure. On the floor was a great pile of washing which I had to deal with, and he wanted each piece to be clean. He fitted a large apron around me, put the water from the copper into the bath and told me to start. There were sheets, pillowcases, shirts, towels and all the rest of the family wash, including all the soiled things which had been used when the baby arrived. He showed me how to do it. First each article had to be soaped, then rolled and left to soak while the next article received the same treatment. When all were soaped and soaked then came the rubbing. A washing-board was put into the bath and I had to rub each piece on the board until it was spotless. As I finished each one my father took a look at it to see whether it was clean or not. If it was not, he gave it back to me and I had to do it again. Then he put the whites into the copper and boiled them. When all the soaping and rubbing was finished then came the rinsing. The bath was emptied into the sink and filled with clean cold water. My father fed the rinsed washing between the wooden rollers of the wringer while I turned its large handle. You who have washing machines and modern gadgets can have no idea of the tiredness and sore fingers which I had on that occasion, when it was all finished. Father rewarded my efforts by telling me he would give me a good hiding if I told what he had made me do. I need not tell you that fear of the hiding kept me quiet, and not until now have I told this story. But I have never forgotten it either!

When I was quite small my father often did nightwork at the wharf where he worked. Two ships came from Scotland, and were known as 'Leith Boats'. One was named 'The Royal Scot', the other 'The Royal Fusilier'. If one ship berthed alongside the wharf the other was anchored out in the river. At such a time the men would have to work all day and all night so that the one could sail and the other come alongside at the next high-water. Nobody refused to work all night, for the men were glad of the extra money. And besides, there were always men willing to take the place of any man who did refuse such long hours. Sometimes Father would come home after working all day, saying he must work all night. This he would do, returning home for breakfast in the morning. There was no day off next day. He would go back and work until tea-time. Imagine it: two days and one night without stopping. No wonder he was grumpy; he must have been tired out. But I loved the time when my father worked this way, for I went to sleep in my mother's bed. There was nothing I loved more than lying with my arms around her. I'm afraid I had little sympathy for my father's tiredness, not realising then what it must have meant to work such hours.

Father came to know the cooks aboard these ships (which carried passengers as well as cargo) and when they berthed he would buy a large enamel bowl of dripping from them. He would bring it home and send me all around the tenements and surrounding streets asking if anyone wanted any. I was given a great many basins to bring home. Father first weighed the basin then put into it a half-pound of dripping. I had to return these basins one at a time so that I did not get them muddled up. For each half-pound I received twopence. Nobody had more than half a pound as this was as much as they could afford. If they had no money then they couldn't have the dripping, for my father would not allow credit. This took me a long time and meant a lot of running up and down the tenement stairs. The profit he made paid for our own dripping. We had the best of it, for there was always lovely gravy at the bottom of the bowl. I thought it well worth the trouble of coming and going, for nothing tasted as good as that gravy spread on our morning toast. Besides, it was free – and that made it all the nicer!

CHAPTER FOUR

MY MOTHER

My mother was a dear gentle person, who loved us all. This even made up for the lack of love from my father. She was small and, to my childish mind, quite beautiful. Her hair was white. I do not remember her ever having hair any other colour. This may have been due to ill-health for she was never very strong. Each year she would have a new baby. This was always a great surprise to us. We would wake up one morning and my father would say 'You have a new brother' or 'You have another sister', as the case might be. I think she had fourteen children altogether, but I am not quite sure of this, for some died at birth and some lived only a few weeks. Five of us survived and I will tell you our names in order of ages. First was Robert, then me, and then came Kathleen, William and Sydney.

We had no bathroom, so each Friday evening after tea, the tin bath, about two feet long and eighteen inches wide was brought into the kitchen and put on the floor in front of the fire. Then we would take turns to have our weekly bath, our knees tucked under our chins so that we fitted in. I always saw to it that I went in first as the water was clean and hot. After each child came out a kettle of hot water was added to warm it up for the next. At last all five of us had been bathed. I loved my bath, for a hot towel would be hanging on the fire guard to dry me with.

We were never normally allowed to lie in bed, not even on Sunday. Only when we were feeling unwell was it permitted. I loved the times when I was poorly, because Mother would come and give me hot bread and milk sprinkled with sugar. It never failed to make me feel better. I think the extra bit of loving helped me as much as the bread and milk.

CHAPTER FIVE

HAIRCUTS AND BRASS BUTTONS

It was an unheard of thing, when I was young, to cut a girl's hair. Only girls with dirty heads had their hair cut. Every so often, a nurse visited the school and if a girl was found to have vermin, or traces of them, she was sent to the cleansing station. (I do not know where this was, but we lived in great fear of going there.) The child's hair was cropped close to her head, and she was given a disinfectant hair wash. This was considered a great disgrace and she would be shunned by the other girls. It was hardly surprising then that every day, without fail, my mother would undo our plaits, and comb through our hair with a small-tooth comb. If we so much as scratched our heads, she would stop whatever she was doing and look to see if we had picked up anything. Each Friday night at bath time she would wash our heads with soda water and Sunlight soap, and then plait it into many plaits. These would not be undone until Sunday, when they were loosed, crimped and shining.

My brothers went to a Jewish barber who lived about half-an-hour's walk away, in Cable Street. He would give them what was called a 'prison crop'. Every bit of hair was shaved off. Needless to say, this was very cold in winter, but the hair took longer to grow if cut this way and that meant it would be a long time before another haircut was needed. For this a charge of twopence was made, and at the end of the ordeal each boy received a little gift, to encourage him to go again. My brother William, having very fair hair, used to look bald when he had his hair cut this way, and much to his disgust the other children used to call him Claudie Whitehead. He was known by this name for a long time.

One day when William was quite a small boy, Kathleen and

I took him to a little park not far from Royal Jubilee Buildings. Now it was the fashion at that time for little boys to wear brass buttons on their overcoats, which were double-breasted and called 'reefer coats'. William had six shining buttons on his coat, and my mother was very proud of them. We played for a long time. When it became warm we took William's coat off and laid it on a seat, forgetting all about it. We saw other children playing near the seat, but did not attach any importance to this. Imagine our dismay when, picking up the coat before going home, we found all the buttons had been cut off. It was a long time before we dared to go home, because we were afraid Father would find out. However, we managed to get the coat hung up on its peg, and we said nothing until Mother was alone. We knew she would be cross, but this we did not mind. I'm glad to say she quietly sat and sewed six black buttons on the coat. Father never noticed that the brass ones had gone. But never again did William have shining brass buttons.

Kathleen and I loved that little park. Each Saturday morning in summer we would try and go there. Our greatest delight was to take off our boots and stockings. We stuffed our stockings into our boots, which we hung around our necks by their laces so that we would not lose them. We would spend all morning running and dancing about in bare feet, making them very dirty. The feeling of bare feet on warm asphalt is something I shall always remember; somehow there was a freedom in skipping around barefoot. My mother would wonder how we managed to get our feet so dirty on Saturdays, but of course we never told.

Some days, before starting off for school, Kathleen and I would ask Mother if we could have a farthing with which to buy some sweets. Now my mother's skirts always had one very large pocket inserted into the seam, and into this pocket went all kinds of things – a thimble, piece of string, a handkerchief and anything she wanted to hide from us children. We would stand hopefully waiting while she felt in her pocket. She would sometimes find a farthing right at the bottom. She would give it to me, with the reminder that I must share it with Kathleen.

We passed a small sweet shop on our way to school. The owner was a most obliging man. He would let us stand and choose whatever we wanted. His sweets were priced four ounces for one penny, so that with our farthing we could get one ounce. When we finally made up our minds we would ask him for whatever we fancied and request him to put it into two papers, so that we each had a fair share. He always did this and we went off to school with half an ounce each. When I see parents giving their children so much money these days I never fail to think of a farthing between two.

CHAPTER SIX

FOUR MEALS FOR FOURPENCE

I do not want the reader to suppose we were an unhappy family. Indeed, my childhood on the whole was a very happy one. Certainly we were poor and my father earned little money, but my mother was a wonderful housekeeper. How she did it I do not know, but we were always well fed, neat and tidy.

I remember how she would send me for twopennyworth of bones, and tell me to ask the butcher 'Would you mind leaving a little meat on?'. I used to come home with a great many bones, which my mother would put into a large iron saucepan. She cooked them until the meat was tender and then left the pan to cool. In the morning there was a thick layer of dripping on the top. This she would carefully remove and put into a basin, ready for our morning toast, which was all we had for breakfast. Next came the bones. These were scraped clean of all the meat, of which there was usually enough to fill a pie dish. With the aid of some of the dripping, Mother made these scrapings into a meat pie. And, my, what a pie that was! It gave seven hungry people a wonderful dinner. Before the next meal I was sent for one pennyworth of pot herbs. For the penny you could have one onion, a few carrots and some turnips. These were cooked, along with a handful of barley, in the juice in which the bones had been boiled. This made a large pan of stew which did for two days' dinner.

Perhaps you can now get some idea of what household management had to be like in my early childhood. In all, those three dinners and a breakfast cost about fourpence. My mother was not alone in her economy. The force of circumstances demanded it. Money was short and appetites were large, so women in those days were obliged to be thrifty.

CHAPTER SEVEN

WATNEY STREET AND MORE ABOUT MY MOTHER

Watney Street was a narrow street leading from Cable Street through to Commercial Road. It was half an hour's walk from home, and we did our weekly shopping there on Saturdays. There were shops on both sides of the road and stalls lined it from one end to the other. In winter the stalls would be brightly lit with naked naphtha lights, and all the stallholders stood by their wares and shouted and called as you went by, trying to get your custom. When she was well enough to go, Mother would take me with her to help carry the shopping home. Her first buy would be the Sunday joint, which was half a leg of mutton, costing 1s. 11d. – she would never pay more. She would ask the butcher to cut a slice off the top, about an inch thick. She called this a cutlet and it was cooked the following morning for our breakfast. She fried it and cut it into seven portions (one for each of us) and served it with a spoonful of fried tomatoes, which she had bought for about fourpence a pound as they were over-ripe.

She bought the vegetables next, including 12 lbs of potatoes at 4 lbs for twopence. She would buy a few halfpenny oranges (we had a half orange each, never a whole one). Then we moved on to the salt stall where a woman would stand sawing up large blocks of salt, which she sold at about 2 lbs for a halfpenny. On we walked, passing the stall where a woman was grating horse-radish. Her eyes would be watering from the strong smell of it. She would sell it at one or two pennies a bag. One shop sold cooked sheep's heads. I could not bear to look at them, but they were considered a great treat. Then there were the 'Rag Girls', as they were called, women with stalls full of other people's unwanted clothes. Usually they had their stalls in a side street where it was a little quieter, and there you could see groups of women examining the clothes, in search of a bargain. I once stood watching Mother while she sorted the clothes over. No article was ever more than a copper or two and on this occasion she was very pleased for she managed to buy quite a large bundle of baby clothes for fourpence. When she got home she washed them and put them away for the new baby, which I only then realised was soon due to arrive.

Soon after the visit to Watney Street during which she had bought the baby clothes, Mother was taken ill. Father called the doctor who examined her and said she must go to hospital. She went to the London Hospital in Whitechapel Road, where she was told she must have an operation for the removal of a tumour. Arrangements had to be made for all of us children to be looked after. Offers were made for each of us to stay with a different neighbour, and Mother then went into hospital. She had the tumour safely removed and stayed in hospital for about three weeks. Then she returned home to await the arrival of the new baby. On our wall we penned a motto to greet her. It said 'What is a home without a Mother'. Mottoes were in fashion in those days. Usually you saw them at Christmas time, but on this occasion it was our 'Welcome Home' greeting to our mother.

A few weeks after this the baby was born. It was a boy and

Mother named him Wilfred. We were allowed into her room to see him. I remember my mother telling me to be specially careful with him. 'He hasn't come to stay,' she said. 'He's only lent to us for a little while.' Wilfred was a poor weak baby and, on thinking about it now, I believe he had no chance of living. When he was six weeks old he was taken into Great Ormond Street Children's Hospital, and within a few days we had news that he was dead.

CHAPTER EIGHT

GREEN BANK

I wonder who was responsible for the name of this steet. When I first learned to read, these were two of the first words I re-member spelling out. 'Green Bank.' Such a lovely name! It summoned up a picture of a cool and beautiful place, covered with grass. Here wild flowers would grow. Here one might lie in the sun on warm days and dream of fields beyond, of quiet country lanes, of birds, of butterflies. The longing for such a place was always with me. I would walk along that street and shut my eyes, willing it to be as I wanted.

Alas, it never happened. When I opened my eyes it was still there – a narrow wretched street full of tiny houses. Each had a small window in line with the front door, which gave straight on to the living room, a room so dark that even on a summer's day you could not see unless you lit a lamp. These houses faced each other across a road which was just wide enough to allow the passage of a horse and cart. On summer evenings people sat on the dorosteps chatting and gossiping until the dark sent them indoors. You must remember that there was neither radio nor television then, and nothing to do when day was done but to sit in the street and gossip. I have no idea how such a street came to have such a name. I only know that it was always a disappointment to me each time I saw it.

CHAPTER NINE

THE MONTH OF MAY

I have fond memories of the month of May, because it was a month in which so many nice things happened. The first of May was 'May Day'. For weeks we had been learning such songs as 'Now is the Month of Maying'. In one verse the words include the phrase 'Each with his bonnie lass is dancing on the grass', and I would think to myself 'Where is the grass?'. However, I loved the song, and I determined that one day I would 'dance on the grass'. At school a maypole was erected in the playground, and some of us danced around it. The girls who were chosen wore white dresses, and as I never had one I was never chosen. Our mothers were invited to come and listen to the singing and to watch the dancing. This was a lovely day for we were given a half-day holiday in the afternoon.

I remember that May 24th was Empire Day. We were taught all the current patriotic songs and had our hair tied with red, white and blue ribbon. Every child had a flag to wave in honour of 'Our Glorious Empire', as it was called. We sang of our lands and possessions overseas. We sang of 'Deeds of Glory'. We sang, and believed we were the mightiest nation on earth. But how many, I wonder, felt as I did. While all this went on I'm afraid I sang with my mouth only, not from the heart. For I saw only those same high walls and thought to myself, 'We sing of our possessions, while not one of us here owns as much as a flowerpotful of earth.' However, a second half-day holiday followed upon the singing, and the sad thoughts of the morning were soon forgotten in the joy of planning what we should play at in the afternoon.

Another event each May was the Catholic Procession, which was held on Sunday in about the middle of the month. There were many Irish Catholic families in Wapping and each made a grotto outside their house. This usually sheltered a statue of the Virgin Mary, with the child Jesus in her arms. It was quite a sight to see one standing in the doorway, surrounded by all kinds of decorations and ornaments. All the Catholics walked through the streets, the girls dressed in white dresses and white shoes, and with a white veil covering their heads and faces. They walked very slowly, singing the virtues and praises of the Virgin Mary. The procession halted at each grotto while the priest went and knelt and blessed it and the people in the house outside which it stood. It was a moving and impressive sight and we would follow and wonder what it all meant. We enjoyed watching it, but what I could not understand (and I don't think I ever will), was that after it had all finished and the grottoes had been taken down, most of the people concerned ended the day by going to the nearest public house and getting drunk, and making merry with singing and dancing. I used to think and wonder how such a moving procession could end in such a way.

CHAPTER TEN

MY FRIEND WINIFRED

When I was not playing with my sister I would go to Winifred's. She too lived in the tenements but on the top floor, six storeys up. In order to earn a little more money many women went daily to offices in the City, where they cleaned and dusted, either before the staff arrived or when they had left. Winifred's mother went office cleaning morning and evening, and every time I went to Winifred's her mother would be setting off for work. I remember how she would say 'Now, Winifred, when your father comes home from work you know he won't feel well. You must be gentle with him and help him into bed.' I thought this very strange until one day I saw why.

Poor man, he worked in the local brewery and drank himself drunk. Only instinct brought him home. He crawled up those six flights of stone steps and knocked at the door. Winifred warned me to keep quiet while she helped him in and coaxed him into his chair. Then, talking to him all the while as if he were a baby, she took off his clogs and socks and led him into the bedroom, where she managed to sit him on the bed and undress him. Then she laid him down on his bed to sleep until the morning. This done, we then played until it was time for me to go home. Winifred must have been about ten years old at the time. I often think of her and wonder if she remembers those days as vividly as I do.

CHAPTER ELEVEN

AUNT AMY

Aunt Amy was my mother's aunt. She thought she was about eighty years old but she did not know the exact year in which she had been born, nor on what day of the month her birthday fell. It didn't seem to worry the old lady at all. She had never been to school so she could not read or write. She was a small fat little woman, with bright black eyes which were always smiling. Whenever she went out she wore a little black bonnet trimmed with jet beads, a short black cape and springside boots. She was a widow, and existed on her old age pension of 2s 6d a week, plus a shilling or two now and then from the Parish relief. She lived in one room, with few comforts other than a small fire grate and a gas ring. Her bed was in one corner.

I used to visit her sometimes, for I was very fond of her. She would visit us too but only when my father was out. She felt he did not welcome her – which was true. Mother would give her any cast-off clothes she had, and Aunt Amy was always most grateful to have them. Sometimes when she came, Mother would persuade her to stay to tea, telling her to take no notice of Father's moods. He did not like her because she took snuff, which he said was a dirty habit. Aunt Amy was the only relative who ever came to see us. I think Father's attitude kept the others away. (Yet Mother never found fault with him; for I think, despite all his funny ways, she loved him.)

Sometimes Aunt Amy would borrow a shilling from my mother. Mother knew that this would never be paid back but she lent it all the same. Aunt Amy would keep away for a week or two after she had been lent money. Then I would go and call on her and ask her why she hadn't been to see us. We all pretended that we had quite forgotten about the shilling and so she would come again. In due course she would borrow another shilling. A shilling would see her over the weekend, and on the following Monday she could collect her old age pension for the week. I cannot possibly see how she managed to live and pay her rent, but there were many like her in those days when I was young.

CHAPTER TWELVE

THE WORKHOUSE AND FATHER WAINWRIGHT

Today the word 'workhouse' is little used, but during my childhood it was common enough. The workhouse was the institution into which old people were put if they had nobody to care for them. Everyone dreaded the thought of ending up there.

When old people became ill they were taken off to the infirmary and transferred to the workhouse when they were better. Everyone there was dressed in a uniform, the men in thick navy suits and the women in thick navy dresses; you always knew where they lived the moment you saw them – their clothes gave them away. I have known many an old person who struggled to exist on a few shillings a week rather than go there. I don't think they were badly treated. It was the indignity of it which was so hard to bear, and even people as poor as these had their pride. I remember my mother being very angry when she heard that a committee had met to consider how to cut down costs. This committee consisted of some of the more wealthy parishioners. One of them suggested that the old men could do without underpants and the old women without drawers. I am happy to say that the rest of the committee refused to do this. Nearly everyone who heard the story completely ignored the offender, for their sympathies were very much with the old people.

If you crossed the Dock Bridge, or lived beyond it, you were said to be 'on the other side'. Neither the grown-ups nor the children 'on the other side', had anything to do with us. They were a community on their own and so were we, although we were all in one parish.

It was a common sight to see Sisters of Mercy coming or going on various errands. These nuns were from St Peter's church, which was on the other side. They wore long black flowing robes and went stockingless. Their hair was shaved off and they each wore on their heads an enormous stiff white arrangement which looked like wings, so that they gave you the impression they were flying. We children called them 'Flying Angels'. In their spare time they sewed and made garments which they sold to the poor at a very low charge. Every year my mother would go and buy Kathleen and me a check gingham dress each, which cost her two shillings. She would bring them home and sew a piece of lace around the neck to pretty them up. Throughout the summer we wore these as our Sunday dresses and they really did look very nice.

The priest of St Peter's was a small man named Father Wainwright. He wore a long shabby black cloak and a large flat felt hat, and always carried a big walking stick. He was very highly thought of by everybody and, although this was a very rough area and drunken fights were often breaking out, if anyone was in trouble of any sort you had only to ask Father

Wainwright to call and he would come. If a child was ill, or a family bereaved he was always there to comfort or help. One day he met a homeless man and took him for a meal; then in a doorway he took off his shirt and gave it to the man. Father Wainwright lived to a great age and he was regarded as a saint by the people of Wapping. In 1967 when I revisited this place I went by his church and on a plaque on the wall I saw his name and history. I am sure there are many like me who still remember him.

CHAPTER THIRTEEN

EVENTS I PARTICULARLY REMEMBER

There were no gardens, trees or flowers in our little community. Most of the houses had a small yard at the back, and the toilet was always in this. We grew up with the streets as our playground. I had a great longing for grass to play on.

There was a small park some distance away but we could not go on the grass because of the notices up warning us to keep off. Now, if you had grown up in conditions like these you might have had some experience of the great longing that comes to a child for the sight of trees and flowers. As I mentioned earlier, Kathleen and I would go to this little park whenever we had the chance.

On going one day I suddenly had a grand plan. I would make a window-box and fill it with lovely flowers! But where was I to get the wood? And where, if I got the wood, could I get some earth? And then, where to get the flowers? I think I must have been a very pushing sort of child because I managed all three. First the wood; I begged an orange crate from a boy who worked for a greengrocer, pulled it to pieces very carefully (for I needed all the nails), then set to work and made the window-box. You never saw a window-box like it in all your life, but to me it was wonderful. The next thing was the earth.

I haunted that little park for days, until finally I plucked up enough courage to ask the park keeper if he would give me some earth.

'But what if I do?' he said. 'How will you carry it home? Earth is very heavy you know.' Here indeed was one thing I had not thought of.

'If I come each day after school with a bag, will you fill it for me?' I asked. He promised he would. So each day I would go with a small bag and he would fill it for me. It took a long time, but at last my window-box was full of lovely earth. Then came the biggest problem. Where were my plants to come from? I decided I would earn some money somehow, but I found that nobody wanted a small girl to do anything. Then, going to the park one day, I met my friendly park keeper.

'How's the window-box?' he asked.

Sadly I told him I could not get any plants. To my great joy he gave me some, telling me how to dig them in and look after them. I shall never be able to describe what I felt when the plants were in the box. By today's standards they were poor things, but to me they appeared beautiful. No plants anywhere were ever tended so carefully or loved so much. Such were the simple pleasures of childhood, which I hope I shall never forget.

Another little story tells again of my love of flowers. I have said a little about my mother, who was never well. One year she had been worse than usual, having had a baby and lost it after a few weeks. I remember how sad she looked and I longed to make her happy. Going through the little park one day I suddenly had an idea. Here were lovely flowers. I would take a flower home to my mother. There were beds of dahlias of many colours, large and beautiful – surely they wouldn't miss one flower. I stood and watched until no one was looking. Then I hurried over the grass and picked a huge bloom. It was bright, bright red. I carried it gently in my small hands.

Suddenly a boy came around the corner. He walked up to me

and asked for the flower, but I would not give it to him. He offered me twopence for it and I would not agree to this either. It was for my mother and nobody else should have it, not even for twopence, which was quite a lot for a small girl to have. I hurried home and gave the flower to her. I cannot tell you who was the happier, she at receiving it or me at giving it, even though I had stolen it. This last bit, of course, I never told her. I said it had been given to me by my friendly park keeper.

I do not remember where I got it from, but one day I found myself the proud possessor of threepence. Mother was ailing still and had to spend the time in bed. I decided to go to the market where we did our weekly shopping and on this occasion I went by myself. I was about ten years old and a true little Cockney child. After walking for nearly an hour, I reached the market. I strolled up and down looking at the stalls, on which were displayed goods of every description. Threepence was such a lot to spend, so I wanted to choose carefully. Then I saw them: lovely peaches! But they cost sixpence each, so how was I to buy one for threepence? I stood and looked for so long that I think the stallholder thought I was up to no good. He asked me what I wanted and I told him that I wanted a peach for my mother, but that I only had threepence. He scratched his head, looked me up and down, then said he might be able to find one which was a bit over-ripe. After thorough searching he held one out to me. Eagerly I took it and handed him my threepence. I cupped my hands together with the peach resting between them and started on my long walk home. In my mind's eye I could see the joy on my mother's face when I gave the peach to her. Then to my horror a boy came along and grabbed the peach out of my hands. Off he ran, and so did I, racing after him. I do not think I had ever run so fast before. My Cockney blood was up and I ran and ran until I caught him.

'*Please* do not squash it,' I implored him.

'Why shouldn't I?' he laughed.

'Oh, please don't! It's for my mother and she's ill. Do give it back.'

He gave it back to me and I raced home with one hand on top of the peach, which by the time I got there was very soft indeed. I gave it to my mother, and great was my delight to see her enjoy such a luxury. I had never tasted a peach, but whenever I see one now that incident comes to my mind.

One year as Easter time came near, I decided to make some hot cross buns. I told my sister and we agreed to give our parents a surprise. So, early on Good Friday we got up very quietly. I was going to make the buns and Kathleen was to help. We had no recipe, but I thought I knew how to make them.

First we had to light the fire so that the oven got hot. This usually took a long time. Once the fire was lit I started on the buns. I emptied some flour into a bowl and put in a few currants, mixing them together with cold water until they made a stiff mixture. I dropped dollops of it on to a baking tin and put it in the oven. We stoked that fire, but the buns would not rise. They didn't even look like buns. By this time we knew that Mother and Father would soon be wanting their breakfast. This thought put me in a panic. I opened the oven door to look at the buns, took them out, burned my fingers in doing so and dropped the lot. My sister and I laughed until our tummies ached. My mother came and asked us what we thought we were doing. I told her of my efforts and asked her where I had gone wrong. Smiling, she reminded me that I had forgotten to put in the fat. This was my first and last attempt at making hot cross buns, but we did have some that day because Mother sent us to the baker to buy a few.

One day, because Mother was still unwell, I was kept home from school to help with the housework and dinner. My mother would give me instructions from her bed and I would clean and dust and make dinner for my father, my brothers and my sister. While I was cleaning I found some pictures, which to me looked very pretty. Now I must first tell you that owing to the vermin which infested the place Father would not allow anything at all to hang on the walls. I was unaware of this at the time, and so I decided to hang the pictures in my mother's bedroom. Its window faced a high warehouse, and as she lay in bed she could see nothing but brick walls. And all day long she heard little but the noise of carts rumbling by, cranes at work and men shouting. I cleaned and polished those pictures, found some nails and hung them up. It made a world of difference to that drab room.

Alas, neither my joy nor my mother's was to last long. On coming home to tea, my father went into my mother's bedroom. I stood waiting for his smile of pleasure. I quite thought he would like my efforts to cheer things up. But no! He immediately took a knife and cut the pictures down, telling me he would have *nothing* hanging on the walls. In vain we protested but, in quite a kindly manner, he pointed out that it was better so, as the pictures would soon be infected with vermin, which would make matters worse than they were already. I saw his point and agreed with him, but I was a very disappointed child that day.

CHAPTER FOURTEEN

MY BROTHERS – ROBERT AND WILLIAM

At this time the streets were very poorly lit at night. There were gas lamps that were lit each evening by the lamp-lighter. He carried a long pole which he used to pull a small chain which was attached to the lamp. Even when lit, these lamps gave a very poor light and we did not often go out after tea.

My eldest brother, Robert, was sometimes allowed to play outside in the evenings. It was a craze among the boys to make themselves carts, usually from a box and a pair of pram wheels. They added a couple of shafts and one boy would sit in the box while another pulled him along. One evening someone had the bright idea of putting lamps on the carts. Now a lamp cost twopence, plus a farthing for a candle. All the boys had one except Robert. On his return one evening, my father noticed that Robert's cart too had a lamp. He asked him how he had come by it. Robert replied that one of his friends had given him the money with which to buy it. Father did not believe him. He put on his coat and took Robert to the boy's house, where he enquired if he had given my brother any money for the lamp. The boy said he had not. When they came home my father made Robert confess to having stolen the money with which he had bought both the lamp and the candle. In vain did he explain that all the other boys had lamps and that he was the only one without one. His words had no effect on Father, who determined that Robert must have a hiding. My mother pleaded with him not to do it, while we other children stood silent, afraid to speak. Finally Mother stood in front of Robert, trying to shield him from my father. This so angered him that he pushed my mother away and took Robert into the bedroom, locking the door after him. He made him strip and gave him a terrible beating with the belt he wore round his waist. I shall never forget Robert's cries or my mother's tears.

He was black and blue with bruises next morning and Mother did not speak to my father for many days after that. Such a hiding for such a small offence! I do not think Robert ever forgave my father. As he grew up there was always a coldness between them and many years afterwards, when Father was quite old, Robert did not even visit him.

So far I have not told you much about my brother William. Well, he was the middle of the three boys, quiet, thoughtful and very fond of horses. Every Saturday and most days during the holidays would find him in the yard of a cartage contractor, where the great carthorses pulled the carts away to their various destinations. The horses first had to be fed and watered, their harnesses made comfortable and their brasses cleaned, for the carmen were very proud of their animals' appearance. William would offer his help in return for a ride, but not many of the men would let him help. He did manage to make friends with one of them and was delighted when allowed to rub his horses down and clean the harnesses. The man repaid him by taking him on his cart. They passed through Poplar, where the carter lived. William was invited to lunch and proved himself to be such a help that each time he had a holiday this particular man would take him with him on his journeys. He would come home smelling of horses, which was most unpleasant, but, as my mother said, it was worth putting up with the smell to see him so happy.

As everyone knows, boys are always hungry – and William was no exception. We had tea at five o'clock and were allowed nothing more to eat until breakfast the next morning. We went to bed at seven o'clock and we never failed to ask for a slice of bread before we went. Mother would gladly have given it to us but Father would not allow it.

One evening after we had gone to bed, William came out of the bedroom into the kitchen where my father always sat during the evening. He said that he wanted to go to the toilet, which you will remember was just off the kitchen and enclosed in a small lobby where Mother kept the vegetables. William found a carrot, put it on his shoulder underneath his shirt and started to walk back to the bedroom. Of course, one shoulder looked higher than the other and my father noticed it at once. Tapping William's shoulder, he asked him what he was hiding. Out fell the carrot! My poor brother had a box round the ears and was sent back to bed in disgrace. In my mind's eye I can still see him, so upset that he cried himself to sleep.

I must tell you of the way we had to dispose of our rubbish. We did not have dustbins as you have today. As I mentioned, in each flat was a tiny lobby which housed the toilet, and in the wall of the lobby was a metal slide which opened wide enough for rubbish to be pushed through. This fell into a large container situated on the ground floor in the great yard below. If you lived on the ground floor, as we did, you sometimes had the most awful smells coming from the 'shoot', as it was called. The container was emptied about once a fortnight and, as the dustmen pulled the rubbish out, great rats and mice would scamper out. Cats of every kind would have a feast on that day.

One day William had been out playing with his friends and I suspect they had raided a van, for he came home at tea-time with his jersey bulging with tomatoes. All his pockets were crammed with them too, in fact he was weighed down with tomatoes. He proudly emptied them on to the kitchen table, telling Mother that they were for her. I shall always remember her look when she turned to William and asked him where he had obtained them. He would not answer her and we all knew that he could not possibly have got such a quantity honestly. I remember that the whole family was in that afternoon except Father. Mother was a very honest woman and would go without rather than take what was not hers. Telling us to watch, she turned to William and asked him to open the slide which lead to the 'shoot'. She picked up the tomatoes one by one from the table and dropped them through the opening of the slide. Poor William! It was a hard lesson, but Mother explained that we must follow her example and never take that which did not belong to us. She promised not to tell Father and we children were too loyal to one another to tell him either.

CHAPTER FIFTEEN

HOW WE SPENT OUR SUNDAYS

Try, if you will, to imagine what life was like all the week. Horses and carts rumbled all day long over the cobbled roads. The cranes on the warehouses squeaked and groaned as they loaded and unloaded the produce from the wharves. The smells of spices from the warehouses, men shouting, ships hooting: all was noise and hubbub. But on Sundays nobody worked. The ships were quiet, the warehouses shut, and the men home with their families.

As I have told you, there were no motor cars. On Sundays the streets were ours, and we could play safely on path or road. We would be dressed in our best clothes and sent to Sunday School both in the morning and the afternoon. In the evening we went to the lantern service. Kathleen and I each had one best dress, which was kept only for Sundays. We wore them to go to Sunday School in the morning, and on coming home it had to be taken off until it was time to set off for the afternoon session, when it would go on again. Returning home it would be taken off yet again until the evening lantern service. We had one pair of black stockings each, of a very poor quality. If they were washed too often they took on a greenish hue, so we had to take these off as well when we were not at church. We had to wear them for seven Sundays before Mother would wash them, in case they went a bad colour. We each had a straw hat in summer, which cost 1s 11d. They were splendid hats, trimmed with wreaths of flowers. Our hair was plaited into two long pigtails all the week, but on Sundays we wore it hanging loose. We both had lovely hair, long and brown, and it looked very pretty on Sundays when we wore it tied with a ribbon. Even the ribbon was put away until the next week.

Our Sunday School was an old corrugated tin building known as the Tin Chapel. Nearly every child went, mainly to be out of their parents' way. I shall always remember trying to sit next to one girl from a rather better-off family. She wore a muff. We did not even have the luxury of gloves, so you can imagine the envy I felt when I saw that muff.

'If only I could sit next to her and put my hands into that muff,' I thought. I did manage to do it once and sat throughout one service with my hands warm inside, feeling like a queen. It is strange how such a small thing stays in the mind, yet things that happened just a few weeks ago are already forgotten.

In my young days, Sunday was observed as the Sabbath, at least by my mother. We went to Sunday School, but could not go out to play. We soon tired of this, so Kathleen and I would each conceal a ball in the leg of our knickers and go further away from home so that we could not be seen. We mostly walked to the Tower of London, bouncing our balls and having great fun as we went along. On reaching the entrance to the Tower, we would hide our balls and walk very sedately through the gate. You passed a 'Beefeater' who let you through if you behaved. Once through the gates, you could see the cannons set at intervals pointing towards the river. These had been used in former days to defend the Tower. We passed Traitors' Gate where, in olden days, traitors were taken through on their way to execution. Then there were the sentries to watch as they marched up and down, smart in their scarlet jackets and dark trousers with a scarlet band down each side. Each wore a very large fur hat called a 'bearskin'. They really looked most impressive. Sometimes we could see the ravens which lived there. You could also see Tower Bridge spanning the river and on the Thames itself were ships, tugs and barges. Once, on a special day, we saw the Crown Jewels and visited the Armoury. Both were closely guarded. We looked as we walked by, but we were not allowed to stop. The Crown Jewels were most beautiful to see.

This then was our usual Sunday walk. We could not stay too long as we had to be home in time for afternoon Sunday School and we were never allowed to miss that. Sunday was for being good, at least that is what Mother told us.

I recall that we were taken one day for a tour of the Royal Mint, which stood almost opposite the Tower of London. It was a very large enclosed building with a small pond in front, which was full of goldfish. We had often watched the fish when on our walks, but didn't dream we would ever go inside the building where all the money was made. (By money I mean coins, for I do not think paper was in circulation then.) Once inside we were amazed to see men stripped to the waist in front of large furnaces. We saw pennies and silver coins pouring into large containers. There was a barrier where we walked while watching this going on. How we longed to be given just one new penny and quite thought they couldn't possibly miss a few. But we were ushered out with nothing, much to our disappointment.

Some Sunday evenings in summer, Father and Mother would go to the Great Assembly Hall in the Mile End Road where services were held. The hall was an hour's walk from home and they went on foot both there and back to save the price of the tram fare. Long queues of down-and-outs gathered outside the hall before the service. They were dirty, homeless people who knew they would be given tea on condition that they stayed to attend the service. For them, starving and homeless, a free tea was indeed a great treat and often they would queue outside the hall all afternoon, waiting for the doors to open.

I sometimes went with my parents to these services, and I would sit and look at these wretched creatures, wondering how they came to be in such a condition. They had to sit up in the gallery, away from the rest of the congregation. Such itching and scratching you never saw. They must have been alive with vermin, so much did they scratch. It quite fascinated me to watch them. The preacher usually spoke of the Love of God and how he cared for all his children, and I often wondered what kind of God he could be that he was content to let these wretches remain as they were. I was only a child but already I was beginning to realise that people fell into different classes: the rich, the poor, and the unwashed. To me it simply didn't make sense. The people in the gallery were the unwashed. Some slept in lodging houses, some in doorways, wrapped in newspaper. Others huddled together for warmth under the railway arches. We would see them shuffling along with all their worldly possessions tied around their necks or fastened to their waists. They looked neither to right or left, for they had no interest in life, and no one cared whether they lived or died.

You may think this an exaggerated description of their condition, but I was there and I saw them. And although I now suspect that much of their plight was of their own making, I know that I was sorry for them at the time.

40

The singing during the services at the hall was very stirring. My father particularly enjoyed it and would return home cheerful and happy. He would sing around the house for the rest of the evening. Then back he went into his shell, and was tired and grumpy once again.

If he did not go to the hall then he used to lie down on the bed for a rest. I clearly remember coming home from Sunday School one afternoon and, forgetting that he was likely to be lying down, rushing into his bedroom for something, singing 'The Cuckoo is a Pretty Bird' at the top of my voice. Before I could get further than the first line I was given a resounding smack on my face. I had woken Father up, and that was unforgivable. Since that incident, whenever I hear that particular song, the memory of that Sunday afternoon comes vividly to my mind.

CHAPTER SIXTEEN

SUNDAY SCHOOL OUTING

The Sunday School outing was the one event of the year which we all looked forward to. You were only allowed to go if you had attended regularly, and as we had never missed a single week we always went. Sometimes we would go to Redhill or Epsom Downs, or even to Epping Forest. It didn't matter to us where we were taken, because it was a day in the country. We had to go to the Tin Chapel the evening before to receive our tickets, which we had to have sewn on to our clothes. It had our name and address on it and if it were not sewn on, we were not permitted to go.

We all gathered outside the Sunday School on the morning of the outing, each with his packet of sandwiches. Two big boys would carry between them a large banner bearing the words 'Wesleyan East End Mission'. Then came the band, made up of a dozen or so boys who belonged to the Boys' Brigade. After we had been arranged in pairs the band would start up and we marched through the streets to its music. Oh, it was wonderful! The day was ours, the sun shone and the band played. Every door was opened and every parent was there to wave us goodbye. You would have thought we were going for a year instead of one day. We sang all the way until we reached the train, and once aboard it we sang again. Nothing could dampen our spirits.

Dear reader, you cannot imagine what a day in the country meant. When we arrived we were let loose in a large field. We always made one wild rush to pick the buttercups and daisies which grew there in abundance. We would fill our hands with great bunches of them, but before very long we threw them away because we had so many other things to do and so many places to explore. There were trees to climb, frogs to catch and, best of all, tea at three o'clock. We all sat on the grass and we were each given a large paper bag containing jam sandwiches, a currant bun, a scone and a cake. Then we were given a large mug of tea. Great was the competition to see who could drink the most.

When it was time to go home, my sister and I would pick grasses until between us we had collected a large bunch. We took this home to our mother, who would welcome it as if it were some rare flower. The grasses would be put into a vase and, believe it or not, kept until the following year's outing, when they would be replaced by a fresh bunch.

CHAPTER SEVENTEEN

STREET CRIES

On Sunday afternoons we would hear the Muffin Man as he came down the street, ringing his bell and calling 'Muffins and Crumpets'. He wore a green baize apron and carried his wares on his head, in a tray covered with a white cloth. These were a great treat on winter evenings when we toasted them in front of the fire. Then came the shrimp and winkle man. Most people would buy something from him for their Sunday tea. Another man came selling celery, which he washed in a basin of water which he carried on his barrow. If it was not washed people would not buy it. Then there was watercress at one halfpenny a bunch and, during the season, mussels would be sold from a barrow at twopence a quart. These in particular were great delicacies.

We did not see these people on weekdays, but we had our daily callers as well. There was a man who came about four o'clock each day selling smoked haddock. We knew him as Swannee, from his cry of 'Swannee Haddock'. His fish was always good and cheap although sometimes it was broken. But then you could not expect whole fish to be as cheap as Swannee's were. Then there were the Italians who made their own ice cream and sold it from their brightly painted barrows, each of which held two drum-shaped containers. Inside one was proper ice cream and in the other flavoured water-ice. Both these were served with a wooden scoop and put on to paper squares, which you held in your hand while licking the ice cream off with your tongue. For a halfpenny you could buy some of the water-ice, and with it went a little piece of lemon. We considered it a great treat even if it wasn't very hygienic. But then we did not think much about hygiene in those days.

Nearly everyone relied on these callers as there were so few shops, but the main reason for buying from them was because their goods were very cheap. I nearly forgot the paper-man: we were all very fond of him. He had a small barrow covered with a roof. It put you in mind of Noah's Ark. Into this barrow he put the Sunday papers. At about ten o'clock on Sunday mornings he would arrive outside the tenements and shout 'Paper!' We children would go and get whatever paper our parents wanted. If somebody on the top floor wanted a paper, the man would send one of us with it and after we came down he would give us a comic which was a week or a fortnight old. We often did this for him because only in this way could we receive a coveted comic. Father would never allow one to be bought, saying it was a waste of money.

These are only little incidents but I hope they give you some idea of things which gave us pleasure. You might think it was not much fun to go up six flights of stone stairs with only an old comic for reward, but even that was enjoyed because we did not walk down flights – we did better than that – we slid down on our bottoms, which was great fun !

Sunday was also the day when the beggars came. They were mostly men without homes, who slept in lodging houses in or around nearby Cable Street. We would hear the first one at about the same time as the paper-man arrived. He came walking in the middle of the road, singing hymns or playing a concertina. Father would never give him a penny, saying 'Let him work. I do.' We children would go and watch him and he would first do the High Street, then every little street and alley in turn so that he did not miss any. Next came a blind beggar with a placard around his neck, stating that he had a wife and four children. He had with him a small dog. This blind man would also sing. Father said he was a sham, only living off other people. Sometimes a woman came, wheeling a pram with two small children in it. How I wished I was rich, then I would have given them all something. Whether or not they were shams I shall never know. I only remember that at the time they had my sympathy.

CHAPTER EIGHTEEN

SCHOOL DAYS

When we were children there were no mixed schools in Wapping. My sister and I went to a board school, which was about a mile from home. To get there we had to pass many wharves and warehouses. On one side of the tenements stood a great tea warehouse. There was a coffee shop next to it with a large sign outside which read 'A Good Pull Up For Carmen'. The men who drive the carts which the horses pulled could get a good meal there. On the other side of the coffee shop was a cork warehouse and next to this was the boys' school. Walking past this one came to a spice warehouse, where all kinds of spices were blended. We always ran by this very quickly as the smells in the air made us sneeze. On the far side was one of the dock bridges. At high tide it was opened to let the ships in and out of the docks.

On either side of the bridge facing the river were large important-looking houses, where the Dockmaster and the other high officials lived. Then came the Rectory and the church with its clock and adjoining charity school, where children were given clothing if they attended church on Sundays and school all week. My mother was too proud to send us to a charity school so we went to the board school. Past the church there were two wharves: one for storing great crates of bananas, and another for sugar. Right next to the sugar wharf was a soap factory. This sent out some very unpleasant odours when the soap was actually being made but most of the time the smells were varied and delightful.

Then at last came the school. It was an old two-storeyed building with a mean little playground and surrounded by tenement buildings. I remember hating school in winter because I was always cold. True, there was always a nice fire in each classroom, but I never felt its warmth because I had to sit at the back of the class. How I envied the girls who sat in front! But only the naughty ones sat there so that the teacher could keep her eye on them.

We had a dear Headmistress, whom we called 'Governess'. I loved her very much for she had been my mother's Governess in her school days. She seemed quite old to me. She was always kind and understanding. After I left school I often went to visit her and she never failed to welcome me.

45

I recall a most unhappy time when my father came to the conclusion that I needed a lesson. Now you may understand, as I do now, how hard it must have been to keep a family of five children neat and tidy. We all wore boots, shoes being only for the well-to-do. It happened that I wore mine out much too quickly for my father's liking. True, I would slide behind the cars as they went along, and kick and dance as any child would, but the fact was I wore my boots out more quickly than did my sister and brothers. One Saturday Father took me to get a new pair. How pleased I was to be getting a new pair before the others! We entered the shop and my father asked for a pair of *boy's* boots to fit me. In vain I cried, telling him I would be more careful if only I could have girl's boots, but my tears had no effect on him and boy's boots I had, fitted with tips and blakeys. As soon as we got home he put the studs in the soles. Oh! the noise they made. I felt terrible. The other children laughed, and I cried myself to sleep for many nights. Those boots would *not* wear out. I kicked with them and I slid with them. In fact I did my utmost to make them wear out, but they would not. At last I grew out of them and they were handed down to one of my brothers. I need not tell you that this lesson taught me to be more careful with my next pair of girl's boots!

CHAPTER NINETEEN

A NEW SCHOOL

I must have been about eleven years old when my mother received a note from my school Governess saying I had been selected to go to a higher grade school as I was considered to be 'bright'. Mother was very pleased for me and set about getting the school uniform of navy gym slip, white blouse and large straw hat, with the school badge on it. The gym slip was meant to reach the knees but my father insisted on it being longer and larger, so that I could grow into it. When I put it on it nearly reached my ankles, but I had to wear it and I felt awful.

On arrival at the school, the new pupils were sent together to see the Headmaster. He asked me to stay behind. When the others had left he told me my slip was much too long and I would have to have it shortened. I explained that my father had said I must wear it this length and that he would not have it shortened. I remember the Headmaster saying 'Poor child' as he sent me to my classroom. I was laughed at by the other children, who were mostly Jewish and came from better-off homes than I did. I was named 'Polly Long Frock'. I found it difficult to concentrate and failed my exams.

At this time Father was out of work and free dinner tickets were given to the children of poor families. One day at Assembly, the Headmaster asked who needed a dinner ticket. Imagine my dismay when I saw I was the only person to put up a hand. I had to walk to the front of the whole school to receive this ticket, which enabled me to have dinner at a centre for poor children, near to the school. I felt too ashamed to go and so during the dinner break I would walk the surrounding streets. I did not tell my mother this but she found out because one day I met a man who knew my father. He asked me what I was doing walking about when I should have been having my dinner. Tearfully I poured it all out to him. He felt very strongly about what I told him, for he was very fond of me. He took me to a nearby coffee-shop where we both had a hearty meal. Later he came to see my parents and told them all about it before going to see the Headmaster to ask that dinner tickets be given in private to children who needed them. This change was eventually made, but I still continued to be a most unhappy child while at this school.

One day, during a lesson on the meaning of words, the teacher – a man – asked me the meaning of a word and I gave the wrong answer. He shouted 'Sit down, you big-eyed coon!' The other children thought it funny, but I felt stupid and unhappy. When I went home that evening I pleaded with my

47

mother and father to allow me to go back to my old school again. Mother went to see my former Governess, who said she would have me back. How happy I was, back among my own kind. I worked much better there, and got very good marks.

Such were the joys and sorrows of my childhood.

CHAPTER TWENTY

THE GAMES WE PLAYED

As I have told you, we had no garden to play in, so we spent most of the time in the streets. As the seasons changed so did the games. In winter Kathleen and I would each have a skipping rope; this was a piece of ship's rope, there being no other kind. How we skipped and jumped through that rope! We took it everywhere with us and had great fun inventing different skipping games. We held hands crossed behind our backs and galloped along pretending to be bus-horses. But when the better weather came we played hopscotch, marbles and gobs and bonsters. We all had tops. The boys would have peg tops which they could spin with the aid of a piece of string. The girls had whip tops which were whipped every few minutes to keep them going. We made the whips from lengths of string attached to pieces of cane or wood.

Then there was diabolo, in which the game was to send a wooden top spinning through the air from a string attached to two sticks. As it came down you sent it spinning up again. This required great skill and I was never able to do it. The best game of all was 'Knocking Down Ginger'. About a dozen of us would get into a line and run quickly along a street knocking at each door as we raced along. We must have been a great annoyance to the people who lived inside the houses but this was our favourite game and never once did we get caught.

In summer when it was hot, the boys would go down the

shoreways and strip off all their clothing and bathe in the muddy water of the Thames. How we girls wished we too could go, but the boys would post one of their number on guard at the entrance to keep the girls away. This was strictly for boys only. They had no towels with which to dry themselves, but cheerfully dried off with their shirts. How we envied them but, being girls, how could we too enjoy this game? There was no answer to this, and the boys laughed to think they had scored over the girls.

CHAPTER TWENTY-ONE

THE CATS AND THE 'CATS-MEAT' WOMAN

I suppose I must have been born with more than my share of sympathy and pity for all living things, and have sometimes let my heart rule my head. But I am as I am and I don't suppose I shall change now. As I have told you, the tenements were infested with mice and rats and everybody kept a cat to help keep these pests at bay. When the cats got too old or they had too many kittens people would turn them out to fend for themselves. Most of them found their way into the great yard which lay behind the tenements, where they lived on anything they could find. People would throw out all unwanted scraps, including fish-heads and the like. The cats were truly starving. Many had mange and sores, and there were always dozens of kittens! I used to look at these poor creatures and think 'How can people be so cruel?' My friend Winifred and I would often talk about these cats and we both decided that when we grew up we would open a Cats' Home. It would be called 'The Winifred Home'. One day I saw a cat with a salmon tin over its head. Someone had thrown it out and the poor creature, smelling fish, had put its head into the tin, and could not get it out again. The poor thing was going quite mad in its efforts to free itself. It never did, because next day I saw it lying in the yard quite dead.

Now I had heard of a place at Shadwell, about one-and-a-half hours walk from home, where unwanted cats could be taken, so each time I could entice a cat into our house I would put it into a large bag and carry it until I reached this place. I would then hand it in saying it was a stray. In this way I took many cats to this place. The neighbours found out and called me 'Queen of the Cats'. Word got around to the effect that if you wanted to get rid of a cat, Gracie would take it for you as a shilling was paid for each cat taken to Shadwell. That was a piece of pure invention on someone's part, and I only took them because I felt sorry for them!

There was no time during my childhood when we did not keep a cat. My mother would regularly put all the boots she could find on a chair beside her bed each night. As soon as it got quiet, out would come the mice; they would scamper about the room in a most alarming manner. Every now and then we would hear a bang and we knew it was Mother throwing a boot at the place where the offending noise came from. This would scare the mice for a few minutes then they would come out again; she would throw all the boots until none were left. Then the nuisance would continue as before. Mother always kept a female cat as these were considered to be better 'mousers'. How we loved our cat. It was always having kittens. After a day or two they were taken away and drowned. This always upset my sister and I. On winter evenings when it was bedtime, I would quietly call the cat into the bedroom. We went to bed together, she purring happily and I stroking and loving her until we both fell asleep.

On looking out of the kitchen window one day I saw a sick cat lying in the great yard. I watched for a long time then I went out with a little milk and tried to feed it, but it would not take any. It lay there, not moving. I felt very concerned about it and wondered how I could make it better. I must have been very young and stupid, but I decided I must help this cat. I would take it to the Children's Hospital at Shadwell. I carefully put the cat in a box, covered it with my doll's blanket and made my way to Shadwell on foot. As you know, we had no transport of any kind. It was such a long journey, but I kept whispering to the cat that soon it would be much better. The box got heavier and heavier, but still I went on until I reached the hospital. I went to the Out-Patients Department and was asked who the patient was. I explained it was the cat and asked 'Could you not make it better?' I think they thought I was quite mad, for they told me they had enough sick children without seeing after cats and if it was sick to take it to a cats' home. So I carried it home again and my mother let me nurse it all evening, but on waking in the morning I found the cat dead. My mother suspected it had been poisoned, but of course we never found out.

About twice a week we would see the 'cats-meat' woman on her rounds. Most people who kept a cat would have a regular order with her for a halfpenny-worth of cats' meat. The woman was dressed in a long full skirt, a black straw hat, and black boots. Around her shoulders she wore a coloured woollen shawl and on her arms bore a large basket in which she carried the meat, cut into small pieces and fixed on to wooden skewers. She charged one halfpenny per skewer. She came along calling out 'Cat's meat!' Many cats, either smelling the meat or knowing the call, followed her as she went along. As she came to each house where she delivered, she got her meat out and fastened it under the door-knocker. I often saw cats jumping up the doors in an effort to reach the meat. People did not bother to take the meat from off the skewer. They gave it to the cats as it was as it took them longer to eat it this way.

CHAPTER TWENTY-TWO

THE CHURCH AND OUR CLERGYMAN'S WIFE

If you walked down the High Street until you came to the Dock Bridge you only had to walk a little further and you came to Church Street. On one side was the churchyard and on the other the church, called St. John of Wapping, with its adjoining school. The church and the school were maintained with money left years before. Standing in an alcove were stone figures of a boy and girl dressed in the fashion of bygone days. The church was old, but quite lovely to my eyes; you walked up about a dozen steps to reach the entrance. On our way to school we could see the time by looking down Church Street. If the clock said twenty-to-nine, we knew we must hurry as we still had quite a way to go.

I had ony been into the church once and knew nothing of how a church service was conducted. One of my friends went each Sunday evening and she asked me to go with her instead of going to our usual Sunday lantern service. I went with her. (Here I must tell you I was always a giggler. I would giggle at the most serious things. I don't know why I did it, but once I started I could not stop.) The service started with the choir boys walking down the centre of the church. They were wearing white robes with a pleated ruff around the neck. I thought they looked very funny and could not imagine why they were dressed in this fashion. Then the priest came into the pulpit. He too had on what seemed to be a large white nightgown. He was a fat man with a bald head and I wanted to laugh, but at that point the singing started and then everyone sat down while the priest prayed. I was most startled to hear the congregation chanting after he had stopped. Then he went on again. This went on and I couldn't understand what they were doing or why, and I started to giggle. I tried to stop, but each time the chanting came I giggled more. While the chanting was going on I could not be heard, but when it stopped and all else was quiet, I still continued to giggle. Everyone was shocked at such behaviour and the priest's wife, a lady called Mrs. Saint, got up and came to me. She took hold of my hand and escorted me to the door, telling me she would come and tell my mother about my shocking behaviour. This she did. My mother apologised for me, saying that it would not happen again and I was not allowed to go to church any more.

I really must say a good word for Mrs. Saint. Before coming to work in the church she had been a qualified doctor. As you know, many people could not afford a doctor and you would not call one in or go to one unless absolutely necessary. Mr. and Mrs. Saint lived at the Rectory which adjoined the churchyard. They employed a maid for the sole purpose of opening the door to the many callers. If anyone in our community had a sick or ailing child who did not respond to treatment at home, Mrs. Saint was the one to go to. We all knew she would advise or help in any way she could. She kept a special room as a consulting room and the hall was used as a waiting-room. It did not matter who you were, or whether you belonged to the church or not; it didn't make any difference, she would attend to anyone who cared to go and she made no charge for her advice (which in most cases was necessary). My mother took my youngest brother to her one day as she could not stop him screaming and, upon examining him, Mrs. Saint told her that he must go to hospital at once, as he had a rupture. My husband when a little boy, was very ill at home, so ill that his mother had to put him in a push cart to take him to see Mrs. Saint. This was on a Sunday morning when she should have been attending church, but she stopped to examine him and said he had pleurisy and must go to hospital. On arrival he was admitted and was ill for many days. I think Mrs. Saint must have been the means of saving many children's lives and I am sure you will think, as I do, that her name was most apt.

CHAPTER TWENTY-THREE

BEANOS

Each year in summer every public house in our community would have its annual outing, known as a 'Beano'. All the year the men would pay into the Beano Club. Then, when the day came, there would be enough money for the treat. This was for men only and it was always held on a Sunday.

At about nine in the morning the brake would arrive. A brake was a vehicle with open sides and a canvas roof which could be rolled back in fine weather. Down each side were forms for sitting on. A pair of wooden steps would be placed at the back of the brake to allow the passengers to climb in. There were four large wooden wheels with iron rims on them. In front was the driver's seat. This was called the 'dickey'. It stretched the width of the brake. Sometimes the brake was drawn by two horses who were harnessed side by side with a wooden shaft in between to separate them. If the brake was large, four horses would be used, two more being placed in front of the first two already there. It required great skill to drive a brake with four horses, for they were controlled only by the pull of the reins held by the driver.

At about eight o'clock we would all gather to watch for the brake. All the men came dressed in their best clothes. Each would have his packet of sandwiches tied with a bright red or green handkerchief. Crates of beer would be loaded into the brake as soon as it arrived, and the men would climb in. The driver would get into his dickey seat and with him came the man who sat next to the driver and who always carried a cornet. When all was ready he would sound a loud fanfare.

This was the moment we had all been waiting for. With a great shout we would all call 'Throw out your mouldies!' The

54

men would have their pockets and hands full of coppers and as the brake started on its journey they would fling them into the roadway. You never saw such a scrambling and pushing in all your life. The children would fight and push, hoping to find a stray copper. My sister and I were always there to watch but I do not think we ever found a copper. We were much too afraid of the big boys. But it was fun to watch from a safe distance. I think this one day was the only outing most of these men had during the year. About eleven at night we would hear the sound of the cornet player as the men returned. Most of them were drunk but they sang and laughed as they set off coloured lights. All declared next day that they had had a wonderful time.

CHAPTER TWENTY-FOUR

HOP-PICKING

Every year in the second week of September many people went hop-picking. Mostly they were women and children; men only went if they happened to be out of work at the time. Nearly all of them went to the Kent hopfields. It was a working holiday but it meant a change of surroundings, fresh air and freedom to enjoy the evenings when the day's work was finished. On the day they set off, the pickers would start out from Wapping about seven in the evening, walking to London Bridge Station, which was about two miles away. They were allocated a special train which left at midnight and there was usually a wait of a few hours on the station.

We would watch them as they went by. The things they took with them would have astounded you. They took pots and pans, bedding, toys, carts, prams and pushchairs loaded with every possible thing which they might need, for they stayed for six weeks. Nothing was provided for them except a truss of straw to lie on.

They slept in barns, outhouses or huts and all day they would pick hops. When meal-times came there was usually a Granny who could not pick but who could do the cooking. A fire would have to be made in the open and the meal cooked on this. Sticks and twigs would be gathered for the fire, and water carried from a well. There were no sanitary arrangements, except a bucket in a hut. It was a very rough life, but these people were tough and knew how to rough it and enjoy it as well. All would be expected to pick, but many children played truant, preferring to go scrumping in the farmers' orchards. And who could blame them, for here were things they never saw in Wapping.

All of them would come home laden with hopping apples, and a little extra money. We never went hopping but I always envied those among my friends who did. What I would have liked but never had was one of those lovely large juicy hopping apples!

CHAPTER TWENTY-FIVE

MY FATHER LOSES HIS JOB
AND GETS ANOTHER

I believe it was in 1912 that Father lost his job. Then men working in the docks worked long hours and received very little pay. Much of the work was for casual labour. We would see groups of men outside a warehouse where a ship had berthed during the night. Here was work for the lucky. Some men were regular, but most or them relied for their work on the different ships coming in to the various docks and wharves and they were paid by the hour. The foreman would come out and beckon to as many men as he needed for the job. The men who were left standing would make a mad rush to the next warehouse in the hope of a day's work. I have seen men who were good friends fight each other for the privilege of getting the job.

Times were hard. The men were dissatisfied. Meetings were

held and the men decided, aided by their Union, to strike for better conditions. This strike lasted for many weeks. The Union ran short of funds, but still neither side would give way. We had no money, no food and no hope. The men were desperate and the Army was called in to keep order. Soup kitchens were opened so that at least the children had one good meal a day. But not so the parents. They managed as best they could.

When winter came some kind friends belonging to the East End Mission gave breakfast to any child who cared to partake of it. Needless to say, every child went who could. The breakfast consisted of a mug of cocoa and two thick slices of bread and jam. We walked for half-an-hour to get it and half-an-hour back, then on to school where we each received our dinner ticket entitling us to our dinner at a soup kitchen. Father was a staunch Unionist and I believe encouraged the men where he worked to stick it out. When the strike was finally settled my father was called to the Manager's office and told he was no longer required as he was considered to be an agitator. This was indeed a blow as he had been there for twenty years. He was blacklisted wherever he went. No-one wanted an agitator. His work-mates avoided him in case they also got involved. Each man was too afraid of his own job to be his friend again. Father was inded a marked man.

I so wanted to help him and then I had an idea. I would write to the Manager and tell him how sorry my father was. This I did, quite thinking all would be forgiven, but I received no answer to my childish letter. Although I hoped and hoped for a reply none came, but eventually Father did get a job.

As I have already told you, there were many public houses in Wapping. In fact I do not think you could walk down any one of those narrow little streets without seeing one. They always seemed to be full of men and women. Children were not allowed in so they were left outside while their parents drank inside. Neither my father nor my mother drank, so this did not worry us children, except on Saturday nights, when there was more drinking than usual. There were no official closing times, so each Saturday night at about twelve o'clock we would be woken up by the noise of drunken men and women coming home from the pubs. There would be singing, dancing, swearing, fighting and drunken laughter. I believe this is why some well-meaning people got together and formed a Temperance Society for the parents and a Band of Hope for the children. Songs were written about the evils of strong drink, and each of the women who joined the Society was given a brooch made into the shape of a white bow, which she wore to indicate that she was teetotal.

We went to the Band of Hope for one evening each week, but we did not need to be told of the misery which strong drink could cause. It was all around us. Children went barefoot and ragged because of it. The few possession these people had went each Monday morning to the pawnbroker to pay the rent. Even Sunday suits and boots were pawned for a shilling or two. This meant that people had nothing to wear but their working clothes, except on Sundays. You see, the clothes went in on Monday and were redeemed on Saturday, so all week long they had to wear the same clothes. Although my mother did not drink she joined the White Ribbon Brigade, as it was then called, just to encourage others to give up this destructive habit.

It was at about this time that Father lost his job. One of the well-to-do ladies who lived on the Pier Head heard about my father and the plight that we were in. Father was offered a job as a labourer with the Port of London Authority. The wages were small but it was work and we were happy once again. As Mother remarked to my father when he told her how little he would be earning, 'Half a loaf is better than none'.

But alas, the job did not last long. Father worked under the other men and one day when they wanted to brew some tea he was sent by them to find some. If you are not familiar with dock life you will not know the temptations which surrounded men on every side. At home you had to pay twopence for a packet of tea, while at work there were cases of it by the hundred. So do not blame those men if they pilfered a bit here and there. Well, on this occasion Father went and pilfered enough tea to brew a pot, and on the way back he was stopped by a dock policeman. Father was sacked on the spot for stealing. In a community such as ours this was indeed a disgrace and it was many days before my mother could bring herself to go out. I think she felt worse than anyone about it. But (as is the way with children) we were soon out and about again, with not a care in the world.

This was what we were born into, and we knew no world outside it. We made our own childish pleasures and were happy.

CHAPTER TWENTY-SIX

LOCAL CHARACTERS

As children we knew everyone around the area where we lived, but I suppose it is natural for some of them to stand out in my mind more than others. I recall that we had one policeman, who kept order. He was a very large man with big feet and a big nose. I don't remember his proper name, but we could always give a name to anybody and we called him Bootnose. If we were doing anything we shouldn't and one of us saw him approaching, we would shout 'Bootnose!' This one word would send us all rushing through the first street or alley we came to.

Then I remember a short, fat man who earned his living by rowing men from the shoreways to their ship, lying mid-river. He owned a small wooden rowing-boat in which he spent most of the day. His nose was very red, with a large growth on either side giving the impression that he really had three noses stuck together. With the cold logic of children, we named him Old Three Noses.

Children can be very cruel when they are small. There was one poor woman who was a widow. She was quite an inoffensive creature, but was nearly always partly intoxicated. She

59

would walk unsteadily, reeling this way and that. She interfered with no-one, but each time we children saw her we would shout at her; we called her Old Mother Born-Drunk. How we tormented her, not realising how cruel we were being!

We had another character who kept a small sweet shop, a surly, grumpy man. He was a cripple and walked with a limp. I expect he must have suffered quite a bit from the remarks of us children. We knew he could not run so we stood at a safe distance and shouted 'Grumpy Lloyd' and by this name he became known. (I hope I do not bore you, but I'd like you to know that I was as naughty as the rest and really enjoyed these childish games.)

I nearly forgot one character that I feel you would like to know about; this was the local chimney sweep. His name was Mr. Kelly. He was a tall, thin man who was a widower and when he was not sweeping chimneys he spent his time in the pub. You may think 'What a lot of time people spent in pubs in those days', but there was no other place for a man to go. The chimneys of the tenements had to be swept every six weeks in winter. So badly built were they that you could not have a fire if you did not have it swept that frequently. The smoke would pour into the room and you were almost choked by it. Mr. Kelly had a standing order to come every six weeks to sweep ours. He would always promise to come early but he very seldom arrived until late afternoon, after the pubs had closed. He would put the rods up the chimney until he reached halfway, at which point the chimney must have curved or sloped for he always had a terrific job to get them to go up higher. Then he would curse and swear and say all manner of things about that chimney. When he thought he had managed to get it through to the pot at the top of the building, he would make us go and see if the brush really was out. His charge for this dirty and tiring job was ninepence.

One day, on hearing him swear so much, I asked him if it made the rods go up more easily if he swore at them. He stood for a while looking at me, then asked me why I wanted to know.

I told him that it was wicked to swear; my mother would not allow us to, so why did he?

'I'll tell you what,' he said. 'When I come next time you remind me not to swear, than I shan't forget.' He came many more times and he would always greet me with 'I'm not swearing, at least not in *your* home!'

Most days in summer and winter we would see the man who played the barrel-organ. This was a musical instrument with two wheels and two handles. The man would push it whenever he wanted to play. When he turned the handles it played the popular songs of the day. On weekdays the songs were gay and cheerful and we would follow him around singing and dancing to the music. But on Sundays he would play hymns and sacred music. He mostly played outside the public houses for here he would collect more money – and that of course was why he played it. I often pitied this man. He was quite old, and very tall and thin. I often wondered where he lived. One day quite by chance I found out.

In those days the Salvation Army women had just started to visit people to sell 'The Young Soldier', their weekly paper. One of these Salvationists called at our house trying to sell us her little paper. I think it cost one penny. This led to her visiting us each week. She would tell us of the social side of the work, which interested me very much. Seeing my interest she invited me to go with her one day to visit an old man and woman who were so poor that she went as often as she could to take them soup, which was made by the Salvationists. I went with her and to my surprise found that the old man was the barrel-organist. He lived in one room above a shop, with his wife, a tiny little old woman, nearly bent in half with age. The room was bare except for an old table, two chairs and an old bed. There were no blankets for the bed. Overcoats were used to cover them in winter. I was very shocked on seeing this and when I told my mother she said 'One half of the world has no idea of how the other half lives.' Whenever I had a chance I would visit this old couple and chat with them. I learned that the man had been a school-teacher in his younger days but ill-health had forced him to give it up. They existed in this one room and he would go out in all weathers to earn a little by playing his barrel-organ. We who are growing old have much to be thankful for, for people care about us, but this couple were only one example of how the old were neglected when I was young.

Jenny had come from Scotland to live among us with her mother, a widow who earned her living by cleaning city offices. Jenny was a lovely girl with red hair and a soft lilting voice. She came to school with us and we loved to hear her speak in her Scottish accent. As she grew older she met, and later married, Tony. Tony opened a fish-and-chip shop just around the corner from the tenements. It was a great success. We had had no fish-and-chip shop before this one and each evening you would see crowds of children waiting for Tony to open. Then they would all crowd in shouting 'a halfpenny piece and a half-pennyworth of chips'. You got a nice sized piece of fish and a paper full of chips for one penny. If you only had one halfpenny you could get a halfpennyworth of 'crackling', the small pieces of batter which fell off the fish as it was cooking. Jenny would serve you with a large newspaperful. Jenny had lots of babies and they would be in the shop with her as she served. If one of her children needed something while she was serving she would keep everybody waiting while she attended to him. But nobody minded waiting, for we would watch Tony cutting the fish and dipping it into the batter. Besides, it was warm in the shop and we had fun with each other while we waited. Mind you, if we became too noisy Jenny would turn us out, so we all knew just how far we could go. Tony was quiet and never spoke to us. I don't think he could speak much English, and that was the reason for his quietness. Jenny's mother would sometimes help with the babies, for she lived there with them. Poor Jenny, I don't think she ever had any time off from serving. Tony did not employ anyone else. She seemed suddenly to become old, then she became ill and died. Tony closed down the fish shop and went away. We were all sorry to see the shop close. Some other people opened it up afterwards, but it was never the same after Jenny had gone.

Charlie was a bachelor about fifty years old, who kept the sweet shop next to Tony. He was rather grubby and untidy and lived with two cats which he allowed to sit on the counter among the toffees. They were female cats and were always having kittens. We liked to go to Charlie's. He would give you good weight for your farthing. He sold egg-and-milk toffee, tiger nuts, Polish nuts, tamerans and such sweets as we do not see today. He also sold hot drinks. He put a small drop of fruit essence into a glass and then filled it up with hot water from a kettle. This was nice, especially in the winter when he would let you stay in the shop with your drink, which only cost you a halfpenny. I think he was glad of anyone's company, for he lived alone in one room at the top of the house. We did not have many shops, but I think Charlie's was the favourite.

We had one baker's shop in our community, owned and run by a German and his wife. They had a family of four children. They baked their bread on the premises and sold it by weight. Each loaf was two pounds. It was weighed when purchased and if the scales showed it to be a little underweight, a nice piece of bread pudding would be added to make the weight up. This we called 'make-weight'; and we were allowed to eat it on the way home. The bread was good and crusty and everybody dealt there. The baker and his family were kindly, homely folk and we all liked them.

One day, after the shop was closed they went for a walk, then for a tram ride to Whitechapel Road to look at the shops. They were making their way back to the tram when they saw a parcel in a doorway. On picking it up they discovered it was a tiny baby girl. They took her home, bathed and fed her and kept her for their own. We were all very thrilled when we saw the baby and ever after she was known as 'Lambie' and lived as one of their family. Yet these were the people who were stoned when war came; these were our neighbours, yet they were cast out because of their nationality.

Life was never dull when I was young. There was always something interesting to see or do. One of my greatest pleasures was to watch the farrier at work. There were many carthorses in Wapping and only one farrier. So every man took his horse there to be shod. The farrier worked in a great open shed. Here he had a large fire, over which he heated the iron until it was red hot. Then he took a large hammer and holding the iron with a large pair of pincers he would hammer it, bending and shaping it until he had made a horse-shoe. Then he fitted it on to the hoof of the horse, who stood by while all the preparations were going on. If the shoe did not fit he heated it again and hammered it into exactly the right shape. Then with another tool he made the holes into which the nails went. When all was ready, he took a hot iron and, lifting up the horse's leg, he would burn the hoof a little to make it smooth so that the shoe fitted perfectly. I used to watch and wonder, thinking that this must be painful to the horse, but I was assured that this did not hurt because the hoof was hard and horny and had no feeling in it of any kind. When shod like this the horse made quite a noise when he walked. As there were a great many horses there was also a great deal of noise! Alas, these are no more. All we hear nowadays is the noise of cars and lorries. The horses were quiet by comparison.

CHAPTER TWENTY-SEVEN

CHRISTMAS AND AFTER

In the very earliest days of my childhood, Christmas was the happiest time of the whole year. Father was in regular employment at that time of my life and always saved for Christmas. On Christmas Eve we would have an early tea before Father took Robert and me with him to Smithfield Market, which was about an hour's walk from home. There we would see turkeys, geese, ducks and chickens being auctioned by stallholders. There were a great many fruit stalls as well and Father would go to each one in turn to see who was selling the cheapest. He usually bought a large turkey which cost about twenty-five shillings. Having got this he would then buy twenty-five oranges for a shilling. Then came the nuts. I do not remember the cost of these but he bought 1 lb. of each. On we went to the sweet stall. There were so many kinds of boiled sweets, all priced at 4 ozs for one penny. He would buy 1 lb. of mixed ones and a box of Turkish Delight. We would wander from stall to stall, sometimes feeling so cold that Robert and I secretly wished we hadn't come, but Father wanted us with him to help carry back the heavy load. We carried a bag each and cheered ourselves up by talking about the next day, which would be Christmas Day.

When we arrived home Mother would be waiting, happy and smiling and with supper ready – a great treat, for it was the one night of the year when we were allowed to have it. Of course we hung our stockings up. Just a stocking, but it held all we would receive. Needless to say we woke early on Christmas morning to look into our stockings. For Kathleen and me there was usually a doll each. Hers had dark hair and mine fair. My father had bought these dolls at the street market which was held each Sunday morning in Petticoat Lane and they cost 1s 11d each. They were lovely dolls, 'double-jointed', which meant that they could move all their joints, including wrists and ankles. They also opened and shut their eyes. But, best of all, they were dressed – even to a hat. The doll was the only toy in our stocking. We expected no more. The rest of the stocking contained a few nuts, some sweets, a bag of chocolate money, a sugar mouse, and at the bottom was a bright new penny.

Breakfast was special on Christmas Day. It would be sausages and tomatoes which had been purchased while at the market. Dinner was wonderful, the turkey with sage-and-onion stuffing, baked potatoes and cabbage. And then came the

Christmas pudding which we had all helped to make weeks before. No puddings ever tasted as good as these.

After dinner we played with our new toy while Father and Mother cleared away. For tea we had celery or whatever had been cheapest to buy at the time, but there was never a Christmas cake. We had never had one and didn't expect it. No Christmas tree either. They were for the wealthy. But we were content with what we had.

In the evening we would gather round the fire while my father roasted chestnuts, which was another great treat. We ate a whole orange each, had one or two sweets and played Happy Families together. You must remember we had to make our own pleasures, for there was no wireless, television, tape-recorder or the like. Our pastimes were simple and mostly make-believe. These indeed were happy days, and I shall always treasure them.

After Christmas, if we had been extra good and helpful and there was enough money left over, Father would take Robert and me, the eldest children, to see a Pantomime. The Panto was held in a Music Hall in Shoreditch. It was called the 'Shoreditch Olympia'. I believe it cost fourpence to go into the Gallery, which was at the top of the Hall and consisted of wooden planks with no backs on them. We climbed many stairs to reach it. It was hard and uncomfortable but we could see everything that went on. There were no loudspeakers or microphones in those days but we generally managed to hear what was being sung or spoken. We saw 'Babes in the Wood', 'Aladdin', Robinson Crusoe' and many others. Once we saw 'Alibaba and the Forty Thieves' but I didn't enjoy that. At one part in the performance the stage was covered with barrels and as the play went on, suddenly the supposed thieves who had been concealed in the barrels, sprang out. This frightened me very much, but my brother was most amused. We loved the Pantomime, the bright lights, the colours and the singing but I never could understand why the men actors dressed as ladies and the ladies as men!

From Shoreditch to Wapping was a very long way. We could have a halfpenny tram ride when we were about halfway home but we always walked all the way there and back, because about halfway home there would be a Hot Potato Man. He had a small barrow with a coke fire, on which he baked potatoes in their jackets. You could get a large one sprinkled with salt, pipping hot for a halfpenny. If we had the tram ride we couldn't have the potato. Father would let us choose which we should have. We always chose the potato and ate it going home. No potatoes ever tasted so good or were enjoyed so much. It meant an hour's walk to have it, but we considered it to be the better buy.

CHAPTER TWENTY-EIGHT

A COUNTRY HOLIDAY

I do not know how it came about, but at school one day we were asked if any of us would like to go to the country for a fortnight. The cost would be 2s 1d each. If we wanted to go we could pay into the penny bank which was held at school. You could pay a penny or more, as you could afford it. My parents consented to my sister and I going and each week on Monday morning in went our precious pennies, until we had enough to pay for both of us to go. My mother patched and altered and sewed until she was satisfied we had enough clothes to last us the fortnight. I think about twelve children went in all. We travelled by train to a place called Childrey. I do not remember what county it was in, but I recall it as a small village consisting of only a few cottages. On arrival at the small country station we were met by a group of country women, who looked us over and then chose which child she would take. I refused to go with any of them unless Kathleen came too. I had been told to look after her as she was younger than I. Now each woman had expected to take only one child and had room for no more. There we stood, refusing to be separated, until a kindly woman came and said she would have us if we did not mind being crowded a bit.

Great was our relief to know that somebody wanted us. She took us home to her small cottage. There was the kitchen in which we all lived, and two bedrooms upstairs, one for her and her husband and one for the children. She had three girls of about our age with whom we shared a large double bed. This was contrived by putting the two of us at the wrong end of the bed. We had great fun sleeping five in one bed.

On the first night we were greatly surprised to see them undress and get into bed with no nightdresses. They in turn were most amused to see us put ours on. They asked us what they were, for they had never worn such things and always stripped all their clothes off before tumbling into bed. Nightdresses were unheard of in that family.

I must not forget to tell you that there was another member of the household: a small lively little dog called Poppy, with whom we had great fun. At our first breakfast there I could not believe it, for there on the table on each plate was a large brown egg. This may be surprising to you, but we had never eaten a whole egg before. Only my mother had an egg in our house and the lucky one among us children had the top of the egg before she dipped into the yolk. So you can imagine how much we enjoyed an egg to ourselves.

The cottage stood in a very big piece of ground, which seemed to us children to begin and end nowhere. There were fruit trees, fruit bushes and so many flowers, which nobody ever tended but which were all beautiful. There were chickens, and a goat of which we were very frightened. We were allowed anywhere in the garden and I well remember finding a large gooseberry bush which was covered with delicious fruit. I sat down and I ate my fill. I think I almost stripped that bush, for here was the first fruit I had ever seen growing. The saying 'Stolen fruit is best' was, I think, most apt in my case. I had never enjoyed anything so much!

68

We were allowed to wander where we would outside in the surrounding countryside. There was something wonderful everywhere. One day we were running along and I was in front when I saw what I thought was a lovely smooth stretch of grass; I raced on to it and great was my surprise to find myself sinking into what seemed to me to be a large lake, but you couldn't see the water for greenery. This frightened my sister and I very much. I scrambled out soaking wet and raced back to the cottage very upset, only to be told to be more careful. I had fallen into a watercress bed.

To start with we had great battles with the local children, whom we called Country Bumpkins while they called us City Slickers. But on the whole they were a friendly lot and once we really became acquainted we were all great friends. On going exploring one day, my sister and I climbed a hill and found ourselves on some rough land, which was dotted all over with little bumps which we were very puzzled about. We wondered what could be the cause of them. Now I always had a very vivid imagination and I suddenly felt certain in my mind what they were. They were dogs' graves and this was a dogs' graveyard, so we must tread carefully round the graves. And for the rest of the holiday we picked wild flowers and went each day to put them on as many dogs' graves as we could. (I have since found out that they were molehills.)

I do not think the sun stopped shining all that lovely fortnight and, as the time came near for us to go home, we heard the news that war had broken out. All the trains were being used for troops. Oh! how we hoped there wouldn't be a train for us. We were told we might have to stay on. But alas we did go home, brown and well.

CHAPTER TWENTY-NINE

MY MOTHER'S HOLIDAY

I was growing up and it was the summer holiday in my thirteenth year. I had been taught to clean the house, to make beds, cook and sew and as I was the eldest girl I looked after my youngest brother, Sydney, who was then a very small boy. He was the baby and we all spoiled him. At this time my father decided to take Mother for a week's holiday to Gorleston, which is near Great Yarmouth. He said I was quite able to keep house and look after Sydney while they were away. I was very pleased to think I was to be in charge of everything, and made up my mind to do the best I could. And so they went on their holiday.

It seemed a very long time, but the day at last came when they returned. I expected to see my mother looking well and happy but I could see she was not. When the opportunity arose I asked her what was wrong. My mother had a gold watch and chain which had belonged to her mother, and she thought a lot of it. She told me she had had a lovely holiday. Father had been most generous. He had insisted that she be measured for a dress, which she was quite delighted with. He took her to shows and paid the Boarding House bill. She couldn't understand how he had managed to save so much. One day towards the end of the week, she asked him how he had managed it. Feeling in his waistcoat pocket he brought out a pawn ticket and showed it to her. He had pawned her watch and chain to pay for the holiday. My mother was most upset about this, and after that each time she wore the dress he had had made for her she would think about the holiday, which had been quite spoiled. It was many weeks before enough money was saved to redeem the watch and chain from the pawn shop. On thinking about it now, I expect my father would not have told Mother if she had not asked about it. I think he expected to redeem the watch and chain and then she would not have known how he had obtained the money. He must have wanted to take her away and this was the only means of doing so.

CHAPTER THIRTY

THE FIRST WORLD WAR

During the First World War food was very hard to get and we went short of many things. Father applied for a job which was advertised. He was granted an interview and told to sign a form. This he did, thinking it would secure him a new job. Great was his surprise when he was handed a shilling and told he was now in the Army. It appeared that each new recruit was handed the King's shilling on joining the Army. He came home most upset for he had never been away from home before.

He was sent to Sandwich, in Kent, and was in the cookhouse there for the four years of the war. Robert also joined up and was sent to France, so only my mother and we four children were left.

There were no ration books and no organised rationing. You just got what you could. We could queue up for an hour for a pound of potatoes, seed potatoes so small they had to be cooked in their jackets. There was no butter or meat for us but sometimes we could get $\frac{1}{2}$ lb. of margarine, which Mother would melt and to which she would then add a meat cube in an attempt to give it a little flavour.

One year at Christmas, there being nothing else to eat, Mother made a large plain boiled pudding which she served to us with some golden syrup (saved for an emergency). I thought it quite funny to be having such a dinner on Christmas Day, but Mother sat and cried as she watched us eat it. We lived on meatless stews, which somehow she made quite tasty.

We had many air raids but there was no damage near to us. On top of the warehouse next to the tenements, there was a searchlight operated by a local man affectionately known as Searchlight Charlie. If he switched the searchlight on we knew there would be a raid. Then we would quickly run down to the Shoreway opposite and look to see if the arms of Tower Bridge were up. If they were, this really confirmed that the raid was expected. Most people would go into the vaults of the wharves for safety, but my mother would not go. She preferred to stay indoors. She would push the table against the wall and we would sit on the floor underneath it until the 'All Clear' sounded.

There was a great hatred for the Germans during this time and many innocent people of German extraction who lived in our community were treated very cruelly. For instance the local baker and his family (of whom I have already told you something). We were all very friendly before the war came, but then they were suddenly looked upon as enemies. Former customers stoned their shop windows and raided their home. I do not know where they went, but life was made so unbearable for them that they left the district.

Those were sad days, for many men went from our little community and so few returned. We were lucky, for after the war my father returned and my brother came home. He obviously had a bad time in France, but he would not discuss it. He said that he just wanted to forget. This was to have been 'The War to End All Wars'. Little did we know what the next one was to bring . . . but that is another story.

CHAPTER THIRTY-ONE

RELIGIOUS MANIA

After the war my father somehow managed to get back into his old job. He was made charge hand and had a few men under him. The wharf where he worked housed many goods, potatoes, tinned fruit, salmon, eggs and rubber goods including boots and plimsolls. These were but a few of the many things stored there.

About this time we were still attending Sunday School each week and the services there were making a great impression on me. I think it was at this Sunday School that I decided I would live a Christian life. It seemed to me that if I could do this all my troubles would be over, for would not God help me in my daily life as my Sunday School teached had said?

I do not know why he began to pilfer but my father started bringing home little things which at first I took no notice of: a few potatoes, a tin of salmon or a tin of fruit. But after a time I began to be most concerned in case he was caught. One day I told him how worried I was. He assured me that they were from spare cases which nobody had claimed and that I was not to worry. He said 'If I do not have them they will be swept into the river. What is better, to take them or see them wasted?' This satisfied me for a while, but I knew it was stealing. Gradually it happened on a bigger scale. I would try to hide the things he brought home, fearing the police might come one day and search the place. I was frightened but I could not tell anyone for fear of giving my father away.

On Sundays a tin of salmon or fruit would be opened and everyone would enjoy it except me. Then I had an idea. I would refuse to eat anything he brought home. Perhaps if I showed him I was a Christian and stood against what he was doing this might stop him. And so one Sunday at tea-time as he handed the salmon round and asked for my plate I said, 'I do not want any.'

He wanted to know why and so I told him I could not eat what I knew was stolen. To my surprise he started crying, saying that he had not thought his daughter would turn on him as I was doing. I felt miserable and in the evening he had a talk with me. He told me that I had religious mania, and that he would have to have me put away if I continued to act in this way. As I did not want to be put away I consented to eat what he brought home, but I felt I had failed as a Christian. This state of affairs lasted until my mother died. I do not know if it continued after my father remarried but I very much doubt it.

CHAPTER THIRTY-TWO

TRAGEDIES

There were many tragedies in our little community and as each one happened we would all sorrow with the family concerned.

The tenements were six storeys high and people who lived on the top floor had to climb six flights of stone steps and walk along six stone passages to reach their homes. Two front doors gave on to each passage, and behind each front door lived a family. A low brick balcony ran along the end of each passage, letting a little daylight into the windows of the flats. These balconies were not guarded and it was quite possible for us children to climb up on to them and look over to the street below. On one occasion a little boy of about five years overbalanced and was impaled on the railings below. On another occasion a little friend of ours fell from a similar balcony, which was at the back of each flat, and he fell into the yard. Both children were killed, yet nothing was done to prevent such accidents happening. Nobody seemed to care, except the sorrowing parents and we neighbours.

Many children were drowned as the result of going down to the Shoreways for a paddle or swim. Some were sucked under moored barges. I do not want to depress you with these stories which I do assure you are perfectly true. I merely wish to let you know how lucky you are, for in this day and age, children have the first priority.

Many new-born babies were suffocated while lying in bed with their parents. Because not many babies had cots they mostly slept in their parents' bed; mainly I believe to be kept warm, plus the fact that there was no room for a cot even if you could afford one. Some small babies were laid for the first few weeks in a drawer into which their small bodies just fitted.

Then there was the added danger from the horses and carts. It was the practice of every child to run behind the carts and to hang on to the tailboard and slide along (this was one of the ways I wore my boots out so quickly!). It was great fun, but sometimes if you were seen by the driver he would fling his long whip behind to shake you off. Many times a child would be trodden under a horse's hooves as in his efforts to avoid the whip he would run off, only to be knocked down by the horse drawing the cart behind. In vain were we warned of these dangers, but I'm sorry to say that we knew no fear and continued as before.

CHAPTER THIRTY-THREE

EPIDEMICS

Every year about September we would have an epidemic. It seemed to go in cycles. One year it would be Scarlet Fever, another year Diphtheria and in my early years it was sometimes Smallpox. Of course, Tuberculosis was with us all the time. I think that most of the infectious diseases were brought about by the conditions lived in.

In the tenements six families used one drainpipe leading to one sink for their waste water. The smells which came from these sinks are indescribable. They were never cleaned and must have been the breeding ground for all kinds of germs. Then there were the rats, which in some cases were nearly as big as cats. And everyone's house was infested with bed bugs, which were most horrible. You would wake up in the morning to find you had been bitten in many places. These bites were very uncomfortable and embarrassing, because everyone knew what they were. My sister and I would rub ourselves with vinegar before we went to bed hoping the bugs would not come near us but alas! they came just the same. Nothing seemed to stop them. I remember my father going round each window frame and doorpost with a blowlamp, burning the bugs which lined the crevices. Mother would go round the beds and mattresses with white vinegar which could burn your hands if you happened to spill a drop on them. But these bugs must have been Cockney bugs. They were tough and nothing could stop them breeding.

One year, during a Scarlet Fever epidemic, we five children caught it and all of us were taken to isolation hospitals in different parts of London. I was taken by ambulance through the streets, and across Tower Bridge to the south side of the river. There, near the Surrey Commercial Docks, I was taken by stretcher on to a pier and from there carried aboard an isolation boat, where I spent the night in a bunk. In the morning I was taken down river to Dartford Isolation Pier and from here to Joyce Green Hospital at Dartford. It was quite an experience but I felt too ill to enjoy it. I can still remember the name of that boat: it was the 'Maltese Cross'. These isolation boats were paddle steamers, kept for the express purpose of transferring infectious people to hospital.

Diphtheria was a deadly disease and if it was not treated in time could kill in a few hours. If one member of the family caught it, in most cases everyone else in that family caught it too. In the case both of Scarlet Fever and of Diphtheria the Sanitary Inspector had to be notified. He would send men along with a van, into which they put the mattress and bedding to take them away for fumigating. Then they lit sulphur candles in the infected bedroom, and sealed the door and windows with sticky tape. The room had to be left unopened for forty-eight hours. You might have thought this process would have killed the bugs too, but after the beds were returned, back they came! People fought a losing battle, for the bugs always won.

If you walked the length of the High Street you came to the gasworks. Mothers of little children who had Whooping Cough would take them to walk about in the close vicinity of the gasworks in the hope of making them sick. It was generally believed that this was good for the child. The smell from the gasworks was most unpleasant and fumy and certainly could in some cases make the child sick. The mothers, in their ignorance, did not mind where the child was sick, as long as it *was* sick, and believed that being sick relieved the congestion on the chest. Once having achieved their aim, they took their poor mite home, only to repeat the treatment until the child eventually lost the cough. In some cases this went on for weeks, and many children were cross-eyed after a bad attack of Whooping Cough. Luckily the children of today have injections before this distressing complaint has a chance to take hold.

Only those who witnessed these unnecessary things can truly be thankful that such things do not happen today.

CHAPTER THIRTY-FOUR

IGNORANCE

The death rate among small babies was very high. As I mentioned, many babies were suffocated in bed. Others were lain on by cats. These cats would seemingly watch for a chance to lie across a baby's face and in a very short time the child would be dead.

When a new baby arrived we would hear people ask 'has it come to stay?' If it lived for a month then you were sure that you were going to rear it. Many of the babies were poor sickly things, with a great dummy always stuck in their mouths. If the dummy fell on to the ground it was picked up and cleaned in the mouth of whoever was nearest before being popped back into the baby's mouth again.

Rickets! You should have seen the poor little legs, bandy and bent, too frail to take the weight of the tiny babies. Mothers would breast-feed their babies until they were two years old in the hope of keeping themselves from having another baby, for it was a common belief that they couldn't conceive while breast feeding. (As far as I know there were no contraceptives at that time.) I do not think people knew how to prevent more babies arriving. This subject was never spoken of in my young days, it was considered a dirty subject and one to be avoided. Many young girls had babies. Certainly most of them were ignorant of the facts of life. I myself was never told anything about babies and when my first child was about to be born I was most shocked to find out how she would arrive. I had imagined my tummy would open to let the baby out. With such widespread ignorance it is small wonder that so many babies died soon after birth.

When a baby was born it was dressed in a fashion very different to that of today. Babies were generally supposed to have weak backs and so a stiff binder about six inches wide was wound about their middle. The binder went round many times so that when it was fastened the child was well and truly encased by it. Then came a long flannel petticoat. This was turned up at the bottom and fastened with two safety pins. It looked like an envelope with its flap turned up and it prevented the child from kicking or moving its legs. Over this went the long nightdress. Plastic pants had not been invented so the child was almost always soaking wet and smelly.

These long clothes were worn until the baby was six weeks or two months old, according to its size and progress. Then they were 'shortened'. Both boys and girls were then put in frocks and petticoats. Boys stayed in these until they were two years old. Then off came the petticoat and dress, and knickers took their place. This was called 'being breached'.

A new baby would always have a veil over its face. What this was for I do not know, unless it was to keep the flies away. We were pestered by flies in summer. People would buy fly-papers and hang them up to trap the flies on. These were long pieces of sticky paper. You saw them everywhere in homes and shops.

If a baby was troublesome, its mother made sugar-teats for it to suck. A small piece of bread was soaked in water and shaped into a ball about the size of a marble. It was coated with a little sugar, put in a piece of rag and tied with a length of cotton. About a dozen would be made at a time and placed on a saucer. If the baby started to cry one was popped into its mouth. I'm glad to say this practice has now stopped. It was so easy for a baby to swallow one of these sugar-teats.

Funerals were a common sight in Wapping. They were always very grand affairs, for no matter how poor a family might be it always gave its members a good funeral. The body was kept at home for a week after the death and put on show for people to see. It had to be displayed for a full week in case people thought you were hurrying the body away. Funerals were horse-drawn. The animals would be glossy and black with long black plumes on their heads and velvet palls hanging on either side of them. The top of the hearse was completely covered with plumes and was attended by bearers in long black coats and tall crepe-covered hats. People from throughout the district would gather outside the house of the dead man and line up on either side on the pavement to give him a good send-off. After the funeral was over and the mourners had returned, a good meal was provided for them by sympathetic neighbours and friends. After the funeral, the family wore black

79

as a sign of mourning, and this was not discarded until a year had passed.

In the case of a very small baby where the family had no money, for a small consideration the undertaker would place the baby in with an adult corpse. Nobody in the dead man's family was any the wiser.

CHAPTER THIRTY-FIVE

LEAVING SCHOOL

I was now nearing school-leaving age and as I had not the least idea of what I wanted to do my father decided that I was to go into service. But this I would *not* do. I wanted to stay at home, where my mother was.

I think my whole life centred around my mother, partly I suppose because she was never well and she relied on me taking her place when she had to stay in bed, and partly because I had a fear of the world outside our community. And so, with it settled that I was not going into service, I left school at the age of fourteen and began the hunt for a job. I was very small for fourteen, with two long plaits of hair which reached to my waist. When young ladies left school they were expected to their hair up and let their dresses down, just to show that they were now grown up. One morning Mother went with me to Aldgate, where we had heard a girl was wanted. It was at an Express Dairy Restaurant and they wanted a 'runner', someone who ran about for the waitresses and at the same time learnt to wait at tables. We met the supervisor who, as soon as she saw me, asked my mother if she was sure I really was fourteen, for I was so small. When she was shown my Birth Certificate she was satisfied as to my age and said I could have the job on condition that I put my hair up. The wages were 6s per week, less 1s 6d for dinners, leaving 4s 6d to take home. Out of this my father gave me 6*d* for my pocket-money. The remaining 4*s* went towards my keep.

The first day at the restaurant was a nightmare. I had to wear a black dress, and a white apron and cap. I tried to put my hair up but it kept on falling down because it was so heavy. The other girls there were much older than I was and were very kind to me. After a little while I was sent to wait on a lady. On reaching the table I recognised the customer as our own District Nurse, a very severe person whom we all feared. I was just as scared of her as anyone else was. I timidly went and stood to take her order. At that moment my hair fell down again. She took not a scrap of notice and gave me her order as if she had not seen me. After that embarrassing episode, one of the other girls suggested that I plait my hair and fasten the plaits along the top of my head. With the aid of a whole packet of hairpins I managed to do this. I continued at that restaurant for a long time and learnt to be a very good waitress.

But at home things were not so good. Mother now rarely left her bed and so it was decided that I should give up going to work and stay at home to look after her and the rest of the family. She had been attending Guy's Hospital and the specialists there decided she should be admitted for an operation to remove a second tumour. She came through the operation well and was home after three weeks. I had to go to Guy's once a fortnight for her medicine, and when she was able she would go to see the doctor.

I always accompanied her on these visits. One day the doctor called me in, leaving my mother to dress in another room. He spoke very kindly to me and asked if I had a father. I replied that I had. Then he said 'Go home and tell him that your mother has cancer and cannot live longer than six months.' I could not do what he told me. I just could not bring myself to tell my father . . . and so I told no-one. I could hardly believe it myself. What should I do? It was just not possible for this to happen. I spent many sleepless nights and could creep into her bedroom in the early morning and watch to see if she was still breathing.

After a fortnight I went back to the hospital and saw the doctor. I confessed to him that I had not told my father that Mother was soon to die. He said that Father must know and I was to ask him to come to the hospital, where he would talk to him. Father duly went. When he came home I asked him if he knew. His reply was 'I don't believe it, and neither must you.' But I did believe it.

And so began long months of anguish and worry. I told Kathleen, and that helped quite a lot. She had now left school and we were very good friends, going around and doing everything together. About this time we joined the Girls Guild which met in the Old Mahogany Bar. This was a branch of the Wesleyan East End Mission and was situated about half-an-hour's walk from home. Our meeting was held once a week, on Tuesday evenings at 7.30. We did Swedish drill, country dancing, played badminton and formed a choir. This one evening we enjoyed very much. Mixing with other girls of our own age we soon made many friends. Tuesday was the one evening which I looked forward to all week.

I had now taken my mother's place in the home and did the weekly wash, cooked, shopped and looked after my father, my sister and brothers. In return my father gave me 1s 6d a week for pocket money, which even in those far-off days was very little. The girls at the Guild would arrange little outings in the summer from which I would nearly always excuse myself, having, of course, no money with which to pay my share. My sister would go and I felt very bitter when she went and I did not. Kathleen was now out at work and earned a fair wage. She paid £1 a week towards her keep, and could afford to buy herself nice clothes. The fact that I was still dependent on Father for mine led to some grumbling on my part, but he said I was quite well off, having 1s 6d and my food and shelter. However, Kathleen started giving me 1s a week out of her wages, bringing my weekly pocket-money up to 2s 6d.

Mother was confined to bed almost all the time, and so life for me was pretty full. I had now got used to the thought that one day we should be without her, but the worry was always there. The medicine from the hospital which I collected once a fortnight contained opium and had the effect of making her so drowsy that she was always half asleep. And when she was awake she did not know much of what went on around her. My father now realised the truth of the situation and sat with her each evening until bedtime, feeling, I think, as helpless as I did. We did not speak about it, but just waited. Time went on and still she lived.

CHAPTER THIRTY-SIX

THE LOCKED MODEL

I found it a hard struggle to make the housekeeping money last from one week to another. Father only gave me £1 10s a week, saying I must learn to be thrifty, and from the house-keeping money I had to pay the rent, which was 7s 6d a week. I also managed to put a little away for insurance. But at least Father always paid for the coal, and we were never without a good fire.

As far as I can remember, my weekly housekeeping budget looked something like the list shown on the opposite page.

The 'special haddock' had to be bought from a shop in Ald-gate called Gowers half-an-hour's walk away. It was cut in two, half each for Mother and Father. We children took it in turns to have the ears. Our bread was dipped in the water in which it had been cooked. We thought it tasted very nice.

There must have been other items which I have now for-gotten, but you can see that after I had done the weekend shopping there was, very little left with which to manage the rest of the week. I would tell my father I had no money left and he would give me some, saying he would have to stop it from the next week's housekeeping. He kept his word, with the result that I was always short, and could never start with a full week's money. I tried desperately to economise but could never make the money last.

My Weekly Housekeeping Budget

	£	s	d
Rent		7	6
14 loaves @ 2½*d* per loaf (2 lbs)		2	11
2 lb. margarine @ 4½*d* per lb.			9
2 tins condensed milk @ 4½*d* per tin			9
12 lbs potatoes @ ½*d* per lb.			6
Meat for week		3	0
4 lbs sugar (yellow crystals) @ 2*d* per lb.			8
½ lb. tea @ 1*s* 4*d* per lb.			8
Sundries		1	0
Fish (i.e. 1 special haddock for Father and Mother)		1	2
Fish – herrings, mackerel or kippers			6
Vegetables – cabbage, pot herbs, beetroots or parsnips			6
Butter – ¼ lb. for Mother			4½
1 new-laid egg for Mother			6
1 lb. plum tomatoes (in season)			1
Milk for Mother and milk puddings		1	1
Egg yolk			6
Gas per week		3	6
Insurance		1	4
	£1	7	3½

I recall most vividly one event in particular, which I think must have occurred at about this time for I remember I was already keeping house. Father used to leave his trousers hanging on the brass knob on my mother's bed. One day I took five shillings from his pocket, hoping he would not miss it. But that evening he asked who had been down his pocket and I had to confess it was I. This time five shillings was also stopped from the next week's housekeeping. At this time I believe he was earning quite good money, but he would never spend any.

In my mother's bedroom we had a model of a house. On opening the front door two drawers were exposed. The side doors revealed more drawers. Father always kept this model locked, and this made me wonder what he had in the drawers. One day when he went out, he forgot to take the key with him. Now was my opportunity! I would see what was inside. Carefully I unlocked the doors and pulled open the drawers. To my great surprise I saw them filled with piles of £1 notes, all neatly tied in packets. I could not believe my eyes. Here were *hundreds* of pounds. Yet I could not have a little more for the housekeeping! Looking at this, I realised that my father had become quite a miser.

I must confess that I took £1 from that pile of money and added it to my housekeeping. The very next day he asked me if I had been to the model as he had left the key by accident. He said he had a little money in it and there was £1 missing. I denied having been there. He believed me, but to this day that £1 note has always been on my conscience.

CHAPTER THIRTY-SEVEN

UNEXPECTED MEETING

One day while I was slicing some meat in preparation for dinner I cut my thumb rather badly. As it would not stop bleeding I ran to a neighbour's house and asked her to bandage it for me. She was very kind, and willingly cleaned and covered the cut. Then she insisted that I went to hospital. She went with me and stayed while I had it stitched. This episode resulted in us becoming friends, and from that day on she would often invite me in for a cup of tea in the afternoons while Mother was sleeping.

She had a large family of girls and boys, of whom I met all but one. While I was there one day a young man let himself in. I was introduced to him, and learned that he was Reuben, the only one of her sons whom I had not met before. He worked on the river and was seldom home. I was most surprised when he asked me if I would like to go with him to see a show. I had never had a boy-friend and was rather shy of boys. But Reuben seemed quiet and almost as shy as I was. Of course, I had first to ask my father whether I might go. He didn't like the idea but gave me his permission.

This was to be the beginning of the courtship with the man who is now my husband. We went about together whenever he was home and I could get away. He asked me to marry him many times but I felt I could not leave my mother now that she was so ill. Three times I gave him up, only to come together with him again. He would say 'Why won't you marry me?' and I would reply 'How can I leave my mother and father, my brothers and sister? Who is to look after them if I go?' But he always replied 'Once you mother is gone, then what will happen to you?'

CHAPTER THIRTY-EIGHT

THE OLD MAHOGANY BAR

My eldest brother, Robert, was now married. I was in my twenties, and Reuben had persuaded me to become engaged to him. Kathleen had promised to stay and look after Mother if I wanted to get married. She was willing to give up her job and take my place, so plans were made for Reuben and I to be married.

I had become so attached to the friends and people of the Old Mahogany Bar that I felt I would like to be married there. I must explain this to you. Before it became a Mission Hall it was known as Wilton's Music Hall. It had been a place of very bad repute, being in the area where many sailors stayed while their ships were in dock. It was a place to which women would lure them. When they had plied them with drink they robbed them of all their wages. The sailors were then dropped through a trap-door and carried, unconscious, along underground passages which lead out into some back streets in Stepney's Highway. When they regained consciousness they of course had no idea how they came to be there. Wilton's Music Hall was eventually closed, and in 1888 it was re-opened as a Mission Hall.

It was situated in an alley called Graces Alley, in the middle of a very rough area. Put to its new use it was a happy place, full of young people who really enjoyed the many amenities offered them. For the boys there was bagatelle, a gymnasium and a band; and for the girls netball, badminton, a choir and a girls' Life Brigade. What happy times we had there! It was one of the very few places in those drab surroundings where happiness could be found. On Sundays there were services which were so bright, with singing so wonderful that you felt you must go. We went because we wanted to. No-one attended against their will. We all dearly loved our Pastor, who was a real friend to all of us. He would often come to visit my mother, and when he knew I wanted to be married at the 'Bar', he arranged for it to be licensed for marriages just for us.

And so, on a day in July we were at last married. My mother got up and was taken to the wedding. But she did not go out again. She died six weeks afterwards.

CHAPTER THIRTY-NINE

THE OLD HOME AGAIN

I have mentioned the Salvationist who used to visit us (the lady with whom I went to see the old barrel-organist and his wife). She was the only person my father welcomed to our home. She was about forty years old and we all liked her very much. She had regularly visited my mother once a week. If Father happened to be in we would all notice his face light up as soon as he saw her. Mother had seen this too and had remarked 'There is your next wife'. How true her words were to prove, for, within three months of Mother's death, the Salvationist became Father's second wife. But she was not as my mother had been, who always submitted to my father's will. Now it was Father's turn to give in to his wife's wishes. She would not live in the tenements and so a house was found in Clapton, where they lived until my father died.

Reuben and I had found two rooms in a Jewish house in Whitechapel, for which we paid £5 key money and a rent of 14s a week. I was not happy there, so when Father decided to leave our old home I applied for the tenancy, and got it. So I really began my married life in the same place as I had spent my childhood.

By the time my father had been remarried for a few weeks Reuben and I had painted and cleaned the old flat and rid it of its vermin. How pretty it looked, with its gay curtains and new lino! We forgot the ugliness of the outside world and rejoiced in the home we had now made together. My mother seemed to be there too, and I felt that she rejoiced with us.

One evening as we were preparing supper, there came a knock at the door. I opened it and there stood Kathleen, weeping. She explained that things were not going smoothly between her and my father's new wife. She begged to be allowed to live with us. Later that evening Father came and asked if she would return with him, but she would not go. So he went back, leaving my sister to live with us. We were very happy to have her for, as I have told you, we were always great friends.

After a day or two my brother William came, saying that he also wanted to be with me. Now here was a problem. How could I put a grown girl and boy in the one spare room we had? There was nothing for it but to do what my mother had done before me: divide the room in two with a large curtain.

And so we were a family again but for Sydney, my youngest brother, who was only fourteen years old and had to stay with Father. As the years went by he was my father's only friend and comforter. For Father once confided in me that he had made a mistake in his second marriage. I think he regretted it to the end of his life.

CHAPTER FORTY

THE PERFECT BABY

We had been married a few months and I knew my first baby was coming. How we planned and hoped. My sister and I knitted and sewed. Never was a baby wanted so much. We all hoped for a girl, but I do not think we would have minded what it was, so great was our joy at its coming.

Reuben returned from work one day with a friend who worked with him on the river. He was a young man who had recently lost his wife in childbirth, leaving him with a little two-year-old son to look after. He met Kathleen and they fell in love. In a short time they were married. So my sister started her married life with a ready-made baby. I'm glad to say it has been a very happy marriage. She has had children of her own and the little boy is now a man, with a wife and family of his own. My brother Robert also found a nice girl and married her.

At last Reuben and I were really on our own. Our baby duly arrived, a little girl whom we named Kathleen, after my sister. I thought, as all mothers do, that she was the most perfect baby ever born. How we loved her! And how I loved to show her off. But I did not want her to grow up in those surroundings. I wanted a garden and flowers and trees for her. I began to hate those high brick walls. I wanted to be able to put my baby in a lovely clean place, not as that place was with its noise and dirt.

As I have said, I was a pushing sort of child, and in growing up I had become a fighter. I would fight for what I wanted and keep on fighting until I got it. I had changed from a timid, shy person into a determined one, with but a single thought in my mind. My children were to have a different life from the one I had known.

CHAPTER FORTY-ONE

I MAKE A CHOICE AND GET A NEW HOME

Kathleen was already a few months old, and each day I would try to take her to the little park in which my sister and I had played as children. There she might lie and watch the leaves as the wind rustled them. There we could get away for a little while from the noise of the wharves and the rumble of the traffic.

On returning home one afternoon I found the street door open. On going in I found that the flat had been burgled while we had been out at the park. Things had been thrown from the drawers on to the floor. The wardrobe had been ransacked and Reuben's best suit stolen. The gas meter had been emptied. In fact anything of any value had been taken. We were most upset about this and though we called the Police we did not find the thief.

The burglary made me more determined than ever that we should get away from those surroundings, but we knew of no way of doing so. A few days later I had an idea. I had heard of a new housing estate which was being developed at Dagenham, in Essex. The developers were the London County Council. I decided I would try for one of those houses so one morning I dressed Kathleen in her prettiest outfit and made my way to County Hall, the headquarters of the London County Council, at Westminster.

It was a very long journey but we made it. On reaching the building I wondered what on earth I should say. I half wished I hadn't gone, but there I was and I would try at any rate. I asked to see the Housing Officer. The clerk wanted to know if I had an appointment. I had not thought of this, but I explained that I had come such a long way and I was sure I could see someone. I was told to wait and after a long time the Housing Officer called me into his office. He was quite nice and started to admire the baby. I knew this was my chance and I said 'She is lovely, isn't she?' He agreed. 'Have you any children?' I asked. 'Yes,' he said. 'Have you a garden for them?' 'Yes, I have.' 'She has no garden. She has nothing! I wonder if you would like to visit the place where I live? Am I asking too much for her? You are building houses. Why can't we have one where we can bring our children up in decent surroundings?' I stopped talking, not quite believing I had said those things, and to an entire stranger. 'Go home now,' he said. 'I'll see what I can do, but this sort of thing is most irregular.'

So home I went, feeling that I had wasted my time. However, a few days afterwards a letter came, together with a form to complete. It was an application for a house on the Dagenham Estate. We filled in the form, and waited. After about a month another letter came, which said that a house was waiting for us.

Then a queer feeling came over me. I wanted to go but I

91

wanted to stay. Here was home. Here were friends and neighbours. Here were the people with whom I had grown up. Suddenly it all became very dear to me. I hated it but now I didn't want to leave it. But I looked at my baby and I knew I must go, for her sake and for others which might follow her.

And so we moved to the new house, leaving behind for ever the old life between high walls.

EPILOGUE

Oh, high brick walls a-standing
So grim and stark and bare
On dirty grimy roadways
You have no beauty there.
Wharves, docks and ships surround you,
All is noise and din.
Can you not see the little child
You mercilessly close in.

Can you not see she hungers
For grass and flowers or trees,
Clean fields on which to play in,
Blue skies above to see.

Oh, high brick walls take warning:
She will not always stay
Beneath your dark and gloomy shade –
Like me, she'll run away.

MY PART OF THE RIVER

INTRODUCTION

I was born in a tenement flat in the East End of London in the year in which Queen Victoria died. My earliest recollection of the world is that it was a grey place; its factories, houses, churches and tall buildings had no kind of colour at all. Even the people looked grey. But these were also the days of the street barrow, where people could bargain for whatever they could afford to buy. Apples, polished until they shone; bright golden oranges, arranged in pyramids; slices of tempting pine-apple, pomegranates; purple and green grapes; bright red tomatoes: all these made a wonderful feast of colour against the dreary background of grey. Added to this were the loud and cheerful voices of the costermongers as they shouted and called to each passer-by to purchase their wares.

The East End was the place to which outcasts and refugees came. From the Tower of London, eastwards, into the densely populated area of Whitechapel, came Jewish refugees from Russia, Germany, Poland and other East European countries. There were also fugitives from Belgium.

The Jewish people opened up small businesses, sometimes using a room in their house in which to conduct it. These people were industrious and hardworking, and during my childhood there did not appear to be many poor Jews. The Belgian refu-gees came during the First World War, when I was a little older. They had fled from the German occupation of Belgium. They were a quiet, hardworking people who opened up the first continental butchers in the East End, for the sale of horse-flesh. We locals took exception to eating horseflesh; in our opinion it was fit only for animals. In most of these shops was a large notice saying 'Not for Human Consumption'. This satisfied us, but the Belgians among us still considered it good eating and bought it just the same!

There were many Irish who lived among us, descendants of the poor who had fled to England during the Irish rebellion and the Irish potato famine. These were concentrated around the docks by Tower Bridge. They came and many were employed in the building of the great walls of the warehouses lining the banks of the Thames. When these were completed they nearly all stayed on to work as casual dock labourers, earning very poor money and living in the most appalling conditions.

From Whitechapel, still going eastwards, one came to West India Dock. Here to the narrow streets which clustered around the docks came the Chinese. At that time you would have thought you had stepped into China, and the area was in fact known as Chinatown. The Chinese opened up small businesses. There were chop-suey shops where Chinese food was served. And Chinese laundries abounded, where laundry was done on the premises and was handed back beautifully washed and ironed. You could find gambling dens there, places of ill repute where men gambled all their wages away, always hoping to make a fortune. The owners of these establishments were most obliging; when a man had no money left, he was politely asked to leave, and was given his tram fare home. Many a man worked hard all the week, only to lose his money this way. I once knew a man who was convinced he could win, but at the end of the evening had nothing left. Not knowing how to face his wife, he went and drowned himself. There were opium houses where the Chinese smoked opium. For a price a man could go and smoke a pipe and get so drugged that he could – for a time – forget his cares and worries. Chinatown was not a place where we liked to go, although the Chinese were the most peaceable of people and did not interfere with anyone.

The East End of London was truly cosmopolitan. Apart from the nationalities I have mentioned, there were Lascars, Indians, Arabs, Turks, Portuguese and many others. Each group of people had their own community and if you ventured among

96

any of them it was as if you were in another country. Each group had its own language and we cockneys were quite shut off from them.

CHAPTER ONE

THE RIVER

The Thames as I remember it was not a romantic river, as many have described it. Those who lived alongside it or worked on it, found it dirty, busy and smelly. It dominated our lives, for our very existence depended on it and there husbands, fathers and sons toiled morning, noon and night, in cold, fog, wind, rain, and sun. The river was no respecter of persons. We watched it in all its changing moods. We knew it could earn us our daily bread; we also knew it could snatch a life if given the chance.

But there was great satisfaction and pleasure, in bathing, paddling or riding on its muddy waters. As I passed over it on my way to school I saw many things which have long since stayed in my memory. Some were frightening: I once saw a drowned child floating, fully clothed (this gave me a great respect for the river). Then I saw and watched, fascinated, a diver going down a ladder from a small rowing boat into the murky depths. Great river rats ran and played on the piles on the foreshore, where they found an abundance of food. Wharves, docks and warehouses lined the river banks, and into these went the cargo from ships from all over the world.

I had only to cross a narrow road and go on through a short alleyway, and there was the river. Here were large ocean-going liners, cargo ships, lighters, tugboats, sailing barges, pleasure boats, paddle steamers and small boats of every description. The river was never idle, and never quiet. The ships had a language which only men who worked on the river understood. For instance, a continuous blast meant 'I am on fire', and three double blasts meant 'I need assistance'. Vessels wishing to pass beneath Tower Bridge and requiring it to be raised gave one long and three short blasts on their sirens (the morse signal for 'B', meaning 'bridge'). Then they hoisted a black ball and pennant at the forestay. In the event of a vessel coming upstream, a telephone message was sent to the bridge from Cherry Garden Pier, advising the bridgemaster that the vessel was approaching. The watchman on the bridge kept a constant look out for vessels coming downstream. River traffic took precedence over road traffic.

Tower Bridge was equipped with four semaphore signals, which looked like railway signals. The footbridges across the bridge have not been used since the First World War, partly because people preferred to wait until the bascules were raised and lowered again rather than climb the many stairs which led up and down to the footbridges. The bascules were raised at the approach of a vessel mainly just before or at high water, so that ships could pass under to proceed to their destination. One of my favourite pastimes as a child was to run up the many stairs at the foot of the bridge then walk across the footbridge and go down the other side. During the War they were closed for security reasons and they have never been opened to the public since.

When Germany sent raiders over London, the bascules were raised, a reminder to us who lived by the river to 'take cover', for it indicated a German raid. A Policeman would ride on a bicycle through the streets with a notice board fastened to him which said TAKE COVER. Most people fled into the vaults of the warehouses for shelter (we had no official shelters) but my mother would never go. She preferred to push the table against the wall, gathering us children around her and give us all a large raw carrot to munch, thus keeping us occupied while the raid was in progress.

CHAPTER TWO

FEEDING THE FAMILY

I had three brothers and one sister, a father (whom I was always at a loss to understand, for he showed us no affection) and a mother whom I adored, for she loved us all. Economy was the keynote of every woman in this community. These women, if they thought up some fresh idea for economising, would run to tell their neighbours so that they too could practise it.

Here are some of the things thought up by my mother. When times were very hard she invented a meal which I doubt had ever been tried out before. She cut a slice of bread for each of us, put each slice in a separate mug, then covered each with boiling water. When the water was absorbed she would pour off the surplus, add a knob of margarine and some salt and pepper and mix it all together. She called it 'Pepper and Salt Slosh' and it was surprising how good it tasted, especially if we were cold and hungry. Then there was Bacon Pudding, another favourite we all enjoyed. With twopennyworth of fat bacon pieces and a small onion, plus a little dripping and flour, she would make a large pudding which smelt delicious. She cut up the pieces, including the rind, and this, together with the onion, went into the basin covered with cold water. The dripping and flour made the crust to cover it with. Then she tied a pudding cloth over it and placed it in a large saucepan and cooked it for about four hours on the top of the open fire. Half an hour before dinnertime she would drop into the same saucepan the potatoes needed for dinner, and in this way all was cooked together.

Sometimes we had a rice pudding, not as I make it today but using water instead of milk. The rice was washed, covered with water and put into the oven until all the water had soaked into it. Then pieces of margarine were dotted on the top, a tablespoon of condensed milk and a little sugar added and a little nutmeg scraped over the top. This was another recipe we all enjoyed. The empty dish was given to the lucky one so that the edges which had stuck could be scraped off, leaving nothing in it at all.

In our house, if we had a relish for tea we could not have jam. We must eat what bread and margarine we wanted with the relish. Jam came out only if there was nothing else. My mother cut the bread and handed it to father, who spread jam on half the slice only (without margarine). He then doubled it over, making a sandwich of it. The same rule applied too with cod-liver-oil-and-malt. Mother was certified as having tuberculosis and was granted a fortnightly supply. She very seldom took it and it was kept instead for us children. Father spread it on our bread in the same way as the jam. It was no use saying you did not like it – you either ate it or went without. Needless to say, we ate it and, surprisingly enough, came to enjoy it.

Sometimes if herrings were in season my mother would buy two at a penny each. Carefully feeling to see they had soft roes and looking to see if the gills were bright red (an indication that they were fresh), she would clean and bone them, then fry them on the top of the fire. When cooked, slices of bread would be waiting and the roe from one was mashed and spread on as many slices as possible and given to us children. The remaining part of that fish was then shared out among us so that we had a portion each. The other herring was halved and shared by my mother and father. We took it in turns to wipe the pan out with a slice of bread. This had all the flavour of the fish and was a great favourite much contested for.

My father when he carved the Sunday joint cut the meat so thin you could have blown it away. It was placed on each plate so that it looked a lot. The batter which went with it was made with flour and water plus a little salt. No egg or milk was used, of course, but when cooked under the joint it tasted wonderful.

The same kind of batter was made for a toad-in-the-hole. Two-pennyworth of strips of mutton, the leavings from breasts of mutton, were placed in the batter and cooked in the oven. Needless to say they were very fatty, but they were greatly enjoyed by us children.

Father hit upon the idea of keeping rabbits in order to eke out his wages. He bought two, a buck and a doe, and made hutches for them. They each had two compartments: one living-room and one bedroom. Each Saturday, Robert was sent around the streets with a bag to collect the chaff which fell from the horses' nosebags. He also collected straw from the stables where the horses slept. We never bought anything for the rabbits in the way of food, but whenever we passed a greengrocer we went in and asked for the outside leaves of greens and cabbages. Potato peelings and carrot and turnip peelings were carefully saved. Stale bread picked up from the streets also helped to feed them.

We children adored those rabbits. Their soft silky fur, their twitching noses, long ears, beautiful eyes and their helplessness made me love them as I have never loved an animal before or since. My father mated them and in due time a family arrived. When the babies grew to a reasonable size, my father would kill one and hang it up for a day or two before skinning it. Then we ate it for Sunday dinner. We children were horrified when Father did this and none of us wanted any. But Father insisted we eat it, saying he could not have good food wasted. He kept rabbits for a long time, and every few weeks we had that hateful meal. One day, about a week after the birth of a new litter, Father went out to feed them, but found them all dead. The baby rabbits all had their eyes out, and the father and mother, each in their separate hutch, were also dead. We all assumed it must have been rats that killed the babies and that the mother and father had died of fright. After this episode, Father never again tried keeping rabbits for food, much to the relief of us children.

Whatever meal was served up, we were not allowed to

grumble. It was pointed out to us that there were many worse off. I expect this was probably true, for my parents were thrifty, while so many others were not.

We never had pocket-money and seldom had sweets. When the longing for some became too great, my mother would make paper squares, put a teaspoonful of cocoa into each and add a teaspoonful of sugar. We were then given a square. This mixture tasted delicious if you dipped your finger in and ate it slowly. When nothing else was available, Mother took a large carrot and cut it lengthways to give us a piece each. This, I am sure, is responsible for the good teeth which I still possess to-day. I remember on one occasion eating some raw carrot and laughing while I chewed it, with the result that a piece got stuck in my throat. I nearly choked – I could not get my breath and went blue in the face. Finally I dislodged it, but ever after I was careful not to laugh when eating carrot.

CHAPTER THREE

HADDOCK, RABBITS AND TURKEY

I remember my mother once buying a large smoked haddock from a street barrow. It was large enough to give us all a share, and if cooked with mashed potatoes would provide us with a good dinner.

Refrigerators were unheard of, as were pantries, and having only one cupboard in the kitchen, in which the haddock would soon have gone bad, Mother hung it on to a small clothes-line in the tiny lobby which, if you lived on the ground floor as we did, led into the drying yard. The lobby led to the toilet and just beyond it was a gate. To keep stray cats out, my father had fixed a frame of wire netting over the gate so that the lobby was closed in, but the air was let in through the wire mesh. Here

Mother hung the haddock, so that the air circulated around it, keeping it cool.

On going into the lobby in the evening, my mother was surprised and horrified to see a large ginger cat hanging on the haddock and the haddock half eaten. The cat, smelling the fish, had bitten its way through the wire mesh until a hole was made large enough for it to get through. Mother called my father, who promptly took a stick and beat the cat unmercifully until it was in such a panic that it ran along up and down the mesh in an effort to find the hole it had entered by. Its fur was torn off on the jagged edges of the mesh, and altogether it was a most pitiful object. When it finally escaped it was half dead. We had often seen this cat in the drying yard and had named it 'Ginger'. Ginger had no home and relied on scraps thrown out by people, so it was small wonder he took the opportunity to eat the haddock. I have never forgotten this incident or the cruelty inflicted on the cat by my father. But then, looking at it from his point of view, all he could think of was the dinner which we had next day to go without.

About twice a week the Wild Rabbit Man came round the streets selling wild rabbits. He carried a pole on his shoulder. Fixed by their back legs to the pole were about a dozen wild rabbits. He shouted, 'Wild rabbits,' as he walked along. Usually one could be bought for ninepence. If you skinned it very carefully and could get the fur off unbroken, then you could sell the fur for a copper or two. The flesh of the rabbit was dark and unappetising and my mother soaked it in vinegar and salt in an effort to make it look a little nicer. If by any chance you could afford a small piece of salt belly of pork to add to it, and then boiled it with onions and with flour-and-water dumplings until it was tender, it made a cheap, nourishing and very tasty meal. Every part of the rabbit was cooked, including the head. The paws were cut off and given to us children. With a length of string attached, these made a toy for us to play with the cat. We pulled it slowly along the floor and the cat, smelling it or thinking it was a mouse, chased around in an effort to catch it. This was great fun. So for ninepence, less the money paid us for the fur, a good meal was enjoyed by all of us and we also had a toy to amuse both us and the cat.

The shops sold not wild rabbits but Ostend rabbits. These had white flesh and clean fur, but were too dear for working-class families. Maybe, if one could afford it, an Ostend rabbit would be bought for Christmas dinner. Stuffed and baked and basted with some fat, these made a meal fit for the gods. But we knew they were not for us, so we cheerfully ate and enjoyed our more humble wild rabbit. And what could have been nicer on a cold winter's day?

During World War One my father joined the army. Food was very scarce – it was a case of getting what you could, for there was no rationing that I know of. Father was an army cook. Knowing how scarce food was, when carving a turkey he carefully put all the breast on one side, packed it into grease-proof paper, made a parcel of it and sent it by post to my mother, intending us to have it for our Christmas dinner. By the time it arrived, the grease had soaked through the paper and the whole package looked horrible. When Mother opened the parcel she did not recognise the contents as turkey and prompt-ly threw it away. That Christmas Day for our dinner we had a smoked haddock which Mother had bought from a street hawker. It was not fresh, but it was all she could get.

When Father came home on leave, he asked how we had en-joyed the turkey. Not until then had we realised what it was. Not wanting to upset him or hurt his feelings, Mother said it was lovely. Looking at us children with a look that defied us to tell, she continued to praise the turkey and to tell my father how much we had all enjoyed it. I am sure she was forgiven that rather white lie.

CHAPTER FOUR

BROWN BOOTS AND BOOT MENDING

To wear brown boots was a thing one never did. Most parents bought black boots, but if sometimes someone better off handed a poor person brown boots, this was looked upon with dismay. Before wearing them they would be dyed or blackened over. If you *did* wear them brown, then the chances were that you would have been met with the cry, 'Brown boots, no dinner!' It was felt that brown boots were a cut above the station in life to which we all belonged, and no one was tolerated who tried to rise above it. This may seem incredible to you, but in the community in which we lived this was always the case.

When in work my father always finished at twelve o'clock on Saturdays. This was the general rule. From midday on Saturday the wharves and warehouses were closed, the cranes silent. If by any chance a ship came and needed to be turned round quickly, some men would go in on Sunday, but they had to work only on the riverside (and not on the river itself), loading or unloading. Usually the men went from the street through a small door which gave directly on the quay, and the wharves and warehouses remained closed until the Monday.

Saturday in my home was boot-mending day. After dinner my father would get out his hobbing-foot. After we had collected all the boots, Father would sit with the hobbing-foot between his legs. It was a heavy rounded piece of wood about two feet high with a slit of about six inches in the middle of its top, into which he put an iron foot. Father had four of these of different sizes. The boots, according to their size, were fitted onto one of these, sole upward. Firstly he had a bowl of water, in which he soaked the leather to soften it. Then, carefully stripping off the worn sole or heel and measuring a fresh piece

of leather, he would cut the leather until it fitted. The smaller
pieces he kept. These would be used to build up the toe or heel
before putting on the new leather. He gathered a handful of
brads before putting on the leather and put them in his mouth.
As he banged them in they came out of his mouth one at a time
until the job was finished. Never did I see two come out together. It was always a wonder to me they did not get en-
tangled in his moustache or that he did not swallow any. I do
not know where he learnt to cobble, but when he had finished
mending a pair of boots it all looked so professional that one
could not tell the difference between his work and that of a
full-time boot mender. He used heel-ball to put on the edges of
the sole. This he would keep warming over a candle as it needed
to be soft before it was applied, being made of a waxy composi-
tion. I was always fascinated watching my father mend the
boots.

When all the boots were finally finished, each pair was
handed back to whoever owned them with strict instructions
not to slide or run behind the carts in them. But, as it is the
way with children, we forgot and continued to kick and slide
and run as before, not realising how hard it must have been to
have so many boots to keep mended and tidy.

CHAPTER FIVE

WASH DAY

Monday was always wash-day. After sending us off to school,
Mother would collect all the dirty washing and sort it into
groups. First came the sheets and pillow slips, then the shirts
and towels, petticoats, dresses, tea-cloths and handkerchiefs
and – last of all – the coarse aprons and stockings and my
father's socks. A zinc bath was placed on the kitchen table, the
copper was lit and heated with wood picked up from the fore-

shore. When the water was hot it was baled out into buckets with a small bowl with a wooden handle – Mother called this the 'copper bowl'. Enough water was carried in buckets until the bath was half full. She added a handful of soda to soften the water and then the washing commenced.

My mother, a coarse apron made from a sack round her and a square of mackintosh pinned over her chest, rubbed each piece with 'Sunlight' soap, giving an extra rub to the very dirty parts. Not being very tall, she had to stand on a wooden box so that she could reach the rubbing board. After the whites were washed, they were put into the copper to boil together with more soda. They were continually stirred with the copper-stick and kept boiling for half an hour. The whole place smelt of boiling washing and steam. After this, they were lifted out on to the wrong side of the copper's wooden lid and left to drain, for the water had to be saved ready for the next boil. The washing was then put through the wringer to extract the rest of the water. The wringing had to be left until the rest of the washing was done as, having only one bath, she could not rinse the clothes until it was empty. Mother struggled to the sink with the bath of dirty washing water and emptied it. Then it was filled with cold water and placed under the wringer. The washing was rinsed once and put through the wooden rollers. If the weather was fine, it would be hung out to dry.

Everyone had a double washing line. From our small window in the kitchen we looked on to a blank wall. At intervals along this wall, standing like sentinels, were tall barge oars. On each oar, one below the other, were pulleys. There were about six pulleys fixed on to each oar, and into the pulleys went the washing lines. These stretched the width of the yard to the pulleys fixed to each balcony, one below the other. The women leaned over the balconies to peg each piece of washing on to the line. Then they pulled the line along through the pulley and pegged on the next piece, repeating this until the first piece of washing was at the end of the oar. Line after line of washing from the ground floor to the top met your gaze when you looked out of the window on Mondays.

If it was a wet day, then the washing had to be dried in the kitchen. For this purpose, Father fixed a batten of wood at each end of the kitchen wall just below the ceiling. He put hooks into the batten and threaded a long length of line through the hooks so that there were lines across the length of the kitchen. On to these went the washing. The ceiling was not very high and most of the time the washing was dangling on our heads. The place was damp and smelly, with steam running down windows and walls. Sometimes in bad weather the washing took two or three days to dry. At length it was taken down, folded and mangled and put back on the lines again to air. Nothing was ironed unless it was absolutely necessary, when a heavy flat-iron was placed in the oven to heat or on its end in front of the fire.

On each packet of 'Sunlight' soap there were the words 'Why does a woman look older sooner than a man?' It went on to explain the merits of the soap, but it was small wonder that women *did* look old at forty. This one day alone was truly an exhausting one, for not only was the washing done but the children had to be cared for, the meals prepared and a thousand and one other things done before the day was over.

When first I was married, my husband and I lived in two rooms on the top floor in a street off the Whitechapel Road. The people who lived here were all Jewish, and were very kind to me. But for some reason I have never understood I felt a foreigner in my own country. I very seldom heard English spoken, for there were many Russian Jews who had come during the Russian revolution. There were German Jews, Polish Jews and many others besides, all speaking different languages. I was shy and sensitive among them, although among my own folk I was as good as my neighbour. The house had no garden, but at the back there was a small box-like yard large enough to hold the toilet. If two people stood in the yard it was a crowd. It was so small, my washing place was on the roof of the house. A large copper fitted into a stone surround heated

109

my water and boiled my washing. The roof was flat with one cold-water tap fitted, and its sides were enclosed with iron railings. Reuben, my husband, fitted drying lines to them for me.

On wash-day I had to fill the copper and light the fire, but first the wood and coal had to be carried up two flights of stairs. An old table served as a bench on which to put the galvanised bath. Needless to say, the view from the roof was wonderful; being so high up I could see for miles over London. But I was not concerned with the view. When it was cold and windy, I stood and did my washing in hat and coat but when the sun shone it was warm and rather pleasant to do my washing in such an unusual place. The washing billowed and blew, drying clean and sweet, for on the roof it was up in purer air.

At the edge of the walls below the railings ran a shallow gulley. Leading from it was a water pipe which carried the rain into the sink in the small yard below. I used to pour all my washing water down it as well, but the roof was flat and prevented the water from running into the pipe. I had to pour it away very slowly so as not to overflow the gulley. One day I tired of letting it go slowly and poured it away in a rush. It overflowed the roof and gulley and poured into the yard below, where my landlady was pottering about. Suddenly I heard shouts, and looking over into the yard below I saw her standing there, absolutely soaked with dirty water. I was horrified at what I had done and quite thought she would give me notice to quit, but she was a nice old thing and forgave me. I was always careful to empty my water slowly after that, for I very much doubt if she would have forgiven me a second time.

CHAPTER SIX

PUDDINGS, THE COPPER AND THE CAT

A few weeks before Christmas the fruit would be bought to make the puddings and on a certain Saturday evening everyone had to help to make them. My father would say, 'Those who don't help, don't get any.' I don't have to tell you that we *all* helped. The sultanas had to be picked over to remove the stalks, the raisins stoned and the currants washed. Then candied peel, complete with sugar, was added. He would supervise us, watching that we did not eat any, but he did allow us to have the candied sugar from the candied peel. Putting all the ingredients into a large china bowl (taken from the washhand-stand), he would mix it all with his hands. Then he filled six basins with the mixture, fixing pudding cloths on and leaving a long length of string on each. On the next day (Sunday) he got up early, lit the copper and filled it with water. As soon as it was boiling, usually about nine o'clock, in went the puddings, with the lengths of string hanging outside so that he could take them out easily. The copper was kept boiling for twelve hours, and the whole place was full of the steam and the smell of Christmas pudding – to me as a child this was a lovely smell.

The copper came in for a variety of uses. It was an old-fashioned copper fitted in the lobby. It was galvanised and set in a stone surround. Its chimney led into our bedroom chimney, so that if it needed sweeping we in the bedroom were nearly choked by smoke.

Each time our cat had kittens, these were placed in a sack and drowned in the copper. At one time we had a cat which had grown old and dirty in its habits. Father decided to drown it. Filling the copper up, he took the cat and dropped it into the water and put the lid on. In its struggle, the cat knocked the lid off and scrambled out. Father ran and caught it and dropped it back in again, putting the lid on and sitting on it. But the cat was not going to drown without a fight. It gave one mighty heave and sent both the lid and my father on to the floor. I think my father felt rather angry to think the cat had the better of him. We children and my mother begged him to give the cat another chance and, being greatly outnumbered, to our relief he agreed.

CHAPTER SEVEN

MY MOTHER'S PETTICOATS

Mother was the central figure in our home. Father worked when there was work available and was head of the household. He controlled the running of it and the conduct and behaviour of the children. We were all a little afraid of him and if we did anything not acceptable to my mother, she only had to say, 'Wait until your father comes home. I'll tell him.' Needless to say, she never did, but the threat was always effective. I write much about my mother, as it was she who was always there, but she had little say in anything, for my father dominated us all.

I remember on one occasion he went to a second-hand theatrical dealer and bought some very showy dresses. I recall two in particular. They were bright-red and white, with wide stripes. The material was thick and warm and Father decided that Mother should alter them and wear them as petticoats. Mother and I set to work unpicking them and then she made them into petticoats. Her skirts reached to the ground and the petticoats were about an inch shorter. Here I must tell you we had no privacy when we washed; we all washed in a bowl at the kitchen sink. Consequently, we all saw what clothing each other was wearing. Mother put the petticoat on one morning and came into the kitchen to wash. My eldest brother, Robert promptly named it 'Bold-E-Figure': you could have seen it miles away. The brightness of it dazzled your eyes, but Mother wore it, as she remarked, 'for the sake of some peace'. I do not recall seeing her in any other petticoats throughout the remainder of my childhood, so long did these last.

On the rare occasions when my parents went out together, Mother usually had a baby to carry. She thought up a most ingenious way of carrying the nappies. Babies needed to be changed often for plastic pants were unheard of. Taking about half-a-dozen nappies, she would pin them one at a time to her petticoat, near the waist. They hung down around her, covered by her skirt. When a dry nappy was needed she took one and changed the baby, replacing it with the wet one. What she did with a full nappy I cannot imagine. I can only suppose this was wrapped up and put in her bag. And what she felt like when all the dry nappies were replaced by wet ones is anybody's guess.

As I grew older, Father suggested that I should become a dressmaker. He said that he would bring theatrical clothes home so that I could pick them apart and teach myself to make dresses. He said he felt I should have a trade to follow when I eventually left school. Although he had his way in most things, and was always obeyed, I refused to agree; the 'Bold-E-Figure' petticoats had put me off second-hand clothes for ever. In vain my father threatened me, but on this one thing I was as obstinate as he was.

He was the only one to have a comfortable chair in my home. It was a tub-shaped wooden chair with railings along the back and sides. The seat was round and in the middle of it were three holes which afforded us great fun. Our cat loved to lie in this chair as it was always by the side of the fire. As soon as the cat snuggled down we children would take it in turn to push our fingers through the holes and tickle it. I am afraid the cat did not appreciate this and on many occasions gave us a nasty scratch for our trouble.

No one could sit in my father's chair when he was home. We always tried to, but were turned out. When resting or dozing he would put a large red pocket-handkerchief over his face, and when he nodded off his breathing would make the handkerchief go out like a ballon, only to retract when he breathed in. This always set me off giggling. Mother would send me out of the room to prevent me waking him up as she knew I would get a hiding if this happened. Always she would say to me 'If you can't make peace, don't make trouble.' I often wish I had let her know how much I appreciated having her for my mother. For a kinder, more peace-loving person I never met her equal!

I never remember my mother without thinking of her pinafores. These were always royal blue with a small white pattern. They covered her from shoulder to ankle and did up at the back, having buttons and buttonholes from the back of the neck. They hung loose from the shoulder and were no doubt made this way to cover her up, as she always seemed to be having a baby. The pinafore always had a large patch at the front. She had a habit of standing at the table to cut the bread and margarine or dripping resting the loaf on her tummy. (She said it was easier to cut if held this way.) Consequently her pinafores always wore out at the front and were carefully patched with the good part of an old one.

The sheets were mended in much the same way. If one wore out, it was turned sides-to-middle and sewn by hand to make it usable again. When sheets were *really* worn out, the good parts were cut away and made into pillow-cases, with tapes on the end. Nothing was wasted. Handkerchiefs were made from the worn pillow-cases and the remaining parts were used as dusters.

On one occasion my mother, who only had one hat (a straw boater), decided she would re-cover it and make it into a new one. Father had bought a large, heavy, black silk petticoat from Petticoat Lane and Mother cut this up and covered her hat with it. It took her two evenings to do it. It looked terrible: she finished it off by fixing a red rose at the side. But she was so pleased with it that no one had the heart to tell her how awful it looked.

Now, my mother had very long thick hair which she plaited into two plaits; these she fastened across the top of her head. The plaits were so long they had to be put from one side to the other until all the plait was used up. She would complain how heavy this felt, so you can imagine the load on her head when she put her hat on. The straw boater had been heavy to start with and added to it now was the weight of nearly a whole silk petticoat, plus the flower and two steel hat-pins to fasten it on with. Nevertheless, she perched the hat on top of her plaits and went out. I went with her. I think she felt wonderful walking out in what she thought looked like a new hat, but before very long she complained of its weight. I persuaded her to take it off. The wind was blowing hard. We were approaching a bridge as the hat blew out of her hand. Before we could catch it, it sailed straight over the bridge into the river. I laughed and laughed, but Mother mourned for that hat for many weeks. We children did not tell her how glad we were to know she could never wear it again.

CHAPTER EIGHT

MEN'S GAMES AND CHILDREN'S GAMES

London was very noisy during my childhood. The carts had large wooden wheels with iron rims and were pulled by great horses shod with iron shoes. These carts made a great deal of noise as they rumbled along, for most of the streets were cobble-stoned. At about six o'clock each weekday morning we would be awakened by the sound of heavy clogs, worn by the men who worked at the local brewery. Everyone in the district in which I lived was working class and nearly all the men wore heavy-soled boots which resounded as they walked along.

Hordes of children played in the streets, shouting and calling to each other. At dinner-time their mothers came out to call them in. Never did you hear such a din, as each mother called as loud as she was able; and as most had quite large families and each child was called by name, the noise was deafening. But for all this, somehow it was a quieter and more human noise than the noise which is everywhere today. Indeed, as a child, I don't think I ever noticed it. It was something we had known all our lives. Yet today I find myself going down a side street and walking the long way round in an attempt to miss the din that never seems to stop.

If you had walked around the quieter back-alleys and streets, you might well have seen men gambling on the street corners. They played 'pitch and toss' with coins, 'crown and anchor' with a board and dice, and various other gambling games. (Football pools were unknown in those days, of course.) The men would pay a man or a boy to be a look out, and he would station himself just round the corner of the street. The moment he saw a policeman approaching he would whistle a signal to the men, who would disperse at once. When it was all clear again, they would return just as quickly and continue the game as before. It wasn't really as much fun as it sounds. Sometimes a man would gamble all his wages away, always hoping that his luck would change, and many tragedies resulted from these games. I once knew a man, who having lost all his wages, went and hanged himself, and I have seen women go pub-hunting for their husbands in the hope of finding them before they had a chance to either drink or gamble their money away. Considering all things, I think it was the women of my generation who had the hardest time. For what with child-bearing, poor housing, unemployment and the constant struggle to make both ends meet, their lot was not an enviable one. Yet surprisingly enough it was the aim of every girl to get married, and those who did not were looked upon with pity and were said to be 'on the shelf'.

Beershops were to be found everywhere at that time. They all did a roaring trade throughout the year and the beer was both cheap and strong. Many men went during their dinner break to buy a half-pint of beer and a pennyworth of bread and cheese, to meet their friends and neighbours and enjoy a pleasant half-hour. In the evenings, the beershops were crowded with men and women. They used to stay until they were turned out, at about midnight, for it was a time when the licensing laws were not enforced. Those who did not wish to drink on the premises had beer served in their own jugs and returned home to enjoy it in privacy. It was a common sight to see children going with a jug to get beer or stout for their parents.

My parents were teetotallers, but I often hung around the beershop doors, listening to the singing and dancing and hoping to get a clay pipe. These were sold for a halfpenny each, but if you stood for long enough and asked for long enough, some man was sure to give you one. We got a great deal of pleasure from these pipes. Mother always saved the ends of the soap and put them in a jam-jar. From time to time she would make bubble-mixture for us by pouring some boiling water on to them. We spent many enjoyable hours blowing bubbles in the street, with half a jarful of this soap jelly and our pipes. Nearly every child had a clay pipe and we held competitions to see who could blow the largest bubble and who could send it the farthest.

If we went to the foreshore and searched in the mud we often found a rough piece of chalk which had been washed down the river or lain on the river bed. This was lovely for playing at hop-scotch. You drew your pattern of squares on the pavement and hopped on one foot in and out of the pattern until you reached 'home'. Each time you hopped over a square without touching the line, you chalked your name on it. It was a simple game but one which gave us hours of enjoyment.

Football was the boys' favourite game. This was always played in the streets not, as you might imagine, with a leather ball but with a pig's bladder. If you went to the slaughterhouse where the animals were killed, you would usually be given one. It was quite large when blown up, the colour of parchment and oval-shaped. The very idea of it now is repug-

117

nant, but in the days when my brothers played football, they played and enjoyed the game as much as the children of today who take the leather ball for granted.

On Saturday mornings, you would have seen dozens of schoolboys, each with a sack, hunting the foreshore or searching in front of warehouses and wharves for wood. When they had collected enough, they went to some quiet back-street or alley and chopped it into sticks, each boy using his mother's chopper. They filled the sacks and would go to each house, offering to sell an armful of sticks for a penny. Everyone required firewood and this was a cheap way of buying it. If you were careful, the bundle would last you a week. It was quite a saving to buy wood this way, for if you went to the shop it would cost you a halfpenny for a bundle that was only big enough to light one fire with. The wood was usually very wet, but if it was dried each night on the hearth you soon had your fire going in the morning. If we could find old orange peel, we dried this too. Added to the wood it make a lovely blaze.

Sometimes the boys would stand at the entrance to a wharf where a passenger ship had berthed, waiting for the chance to carry luggage for a penny or two. Often they would bring their homemade carts along to make their job easier, for the journey from the ship to the railway station was at least half-an-hour's walk.

At a certain wharf about once a week we saw cart-loads of scrap tin being taken in before being transferred to a German ship. Once taken to Germany it was treated and remade into toys, such as small engines and trains. These toys were then shipped back to England and sold for about sixpence each. We knew it was English tin because often, if we turned the toy upside down, the original English tin-maker's name was still stamped on it. Tate or Lyle syrup tins were often used. To us as children this seemed a silly way of going on: the Germans bought our scrap and we bought toys from them made from the scrap we had sold them.

Toys then were very poor and cheap by today's standards.

One could buy a doll's china tea-set for 6¾d and a baby doll cost you the same. A box of wooden-cube bricks, complete with pictures, cost 6¾d as well, and a clockwork train set cost 1s 11¾d. Even at these prices, they were too dear for the likes of us. The only toys we possessed were those given to us at Christmas time. You will notice that the prices of all toys included an odd three-farthings. In my mother's opinion, it made it sound much cheaper than the round figure and she thought this was the reason why, for example, gingham was sold at 4¾d per yard, calico at 6¾d per yard, and a pair of sheets sold for 1s 11¾d. You were very seldom given the farthing change but offered a bundle of hairpins or a packet of dress-making pins in lieu.

CHAPTER NINE

SMUGGLERS AND TUNNELS

At one time Wapping was a most notorious place, where murder and smuggling abounded. When I was small I visited a large mansion which in former days had been used for smuggling. In the grounds was a sunken garden which was approached by way of a spiral staircase. This led to an enclosed yard deep beneath the ground. In it was an iron door. On entering through it one found oneself in a dark passage which led to the river bank and another solid iron door, which could only be seen at low tide. This was one of the many ways used to smuggle goods into Wapping. The mansion was situated in Black-Boy Alley, a most unusual place for such a building.

Below the bed of the river at Wapping Station was the famous tunnel, two miles long, by which the East London Railway passed under to Rotherhithe. It was the first tunnel constructed by Brunel under the Thames. A little further on was another tunnel, this one for pedestrians, beneath Shadwell and Rotherhithe. When on holiday from school I remember going down hundreds of spiral stairs until I reached the tunnel. The walls were all white tiles and here and there a trickle of water would flow out, reminding me I was beneath the Thames. Then I would run as fast as my legs would carry me until I reached halfway, where there was daylight, for a flight of stairs led up to Rotherhithe. On I would run until I reached the end of the tunnel.

My destination was Southwark Park, which was across the road from the mouth of the tunnel. This was a large open space laid out as a park where children were free to play on the grass. We had no such place where I lived. True, there was a small recreation ground, but we had to keep to the paths. In Southwark Park we were free to run and jump on the grass to our heart's content. When we tired of the grass there was always the sand pit, which my Mother said was lousy (for we never went there but we came home with more than we had gone with). To us as children, Southwark Park was heaven. With sandwiches of bread and jam and a bottle of water we would spend a whole day there. The run through the dreaded tunnel was well worth doing when one could spend a happy day as free as the air.

CHAPTER TEN

SUNDAY AFTERNOONS

Try, if you can, to visualise a cobblestone road with high warehouses on one side and high tenement buildings opposite. Imagine it is empty: no cars, no motor-bikes, no pedestrians. The water-cart has just been and the road is clean. In each warehouse wall is a loophole just high enough for children to climb into. It is Sunday. Mothers and fathers are having their Sunday afternoon sleep and the children have been sent out; some to Sunday School, some to play, anywhere as long as they are out. Most are playing in the loopholes.

Two young women come out carrying a large heavy ship's

rope. One crosses to the other side of the road. They each hold an end of the rope. Then they begin to turn the rope. Immediately the children jump down from the loopholes and form a crocodile. The fun begins. They jump in and out of the circle made by the turning rope and must 'keep the pot boiling'; not one must miss. Big boys, big girls, and the little ones too – all are included. When this game finishes, everyone jumps in to the circle and sings the rhyme:

> 'All in together, cold frosty weather,
> When the wind blows we all go together.
> I saw Peter looking out the window.
> Caroline, Caroline. Shoot! Bang! Fire!'

On the word 'Fire' we all jump out.

I do not know where this rhyme originated but there were many others which we used to sing when we were skipping one at a time. Two girls turned the rope, while one girl took her turn at skipping. The girls who turned the rope sang as they turned. The skipper had to skip the whole tune through. If she stopped the rope she was out and the next girl took her turn. These are three of the rhymes to which we skipped:

> I'll tell Mother when I go home,
> The boys won't let the girls alone.

> They've pulled my hair and broke my comb,
> I'll tell Mother when I go home.

> I'm going to London next Sunday morning,
> I'm going to London at half-past ten,

> Give my love to the dear old doctor,
> Tell him I can't stay here any longer.

> Hi, Hi, here we go,
> The driver's drunk and the horse won't go.

> Now we're going back, now we're going back,
> Back to the place where we get more grub.

When we get there, when we get there,
See our hair grow longer.

I am a little beggar-girl, my mother she is dead,
My father is a drunkard and won't give me no bread.

I look out of the window and hear the organ play,
God bless my dear Mother, she's gone so far away.

Ding Dong my castle bell, Farewell my Mother,
I'll be buried in the old Churchyard by the side of my dear
  Mother.

My coffin shall be black, six white angels at my back,
Two to watch and two to pray and two to carry my soul away.

The wind blows high, the grass grows green.
All the boys they love us, excepting Gracie Platt.
She's so pretty, she's the pride of London City,
She can play the hornpipe, one, two, three,
She's the fairest lady.

(I put my name only as an example. The girl whose turn it was
used her name.)

These songs and others rang in the streets as we played, and
the sound of them joined with the clatter of hoops rolling on
the cobblestones (the boys' were made of iron and the girls' of
wood) and the noise of homemade stilts clonking along. Sounds
of laughter and of tears mingled and filled the air. I have never
seen a whole community of young people enjoying themselves
as much as we did on Sunday afternoons. Have you imagined
it? Not a toot from a car, not a sign of any traffic. For this was
Sunday, a day when nobody worked.

At about five o'clock the rope was taken indoors and the
children all went home for tea. Sunday tea was an occasion.

On Sundays a tablecloth was laid. (Many families had newspaper on the table all the week, but never on Sunday.) The tea consisted of a pint of winkles or shrimps with bread and margarine, and a cup of tea. These were eaten with great relish. Not a feast, you might think, but then you were not there to enjoy them. Winkles were my greatest delight, until one day I was told that they fed on dead bodies in the sea. This put me off winkles for ever.

After tea, each child was sent out again, this time to listen to the open air service, which was held in the street where we had played our skipping games. Not far away was a small mission hall, and it was from there that the band of about half-a-dozen workers came with hymn books, stool and harmonium. The preacher, a man of eighty years, and his forty-year-old hunchback daughter led the service. The daughter played the harmonium, the hymn was announced, books were given out and we all sang 'Onward Christian Soldiers'. Windows were flung open and people leaned out, listening to the singing. When the hymn finished, the old man prayed and men bared their heads. The same men who in the week cursed God Almighty, men who swore dreadful oaths, now stood reverent and bare headed, listening to the pleading of this old man as he beseeched God to forgive men in their sins. When the prayer finished, we sang 'Fight the Good Fight'.

I wish you could have been there, for this was a sight so moving to see: the deserted road, the closed wharves and warehouses, the people standing or watching from their houses, none of whom had two halfpennies for a penny; some who would tomorrow have to pawn their belongings before they could get a meal; some with no work to go to. And yet they could all sing, and listen while the old man gave his sermon. I can see him now, tall, thin and bald, with flowing white beard and a voice that could be heard from one end of the street to the other. He warned us of Hell Fire, of the Wrath of God and of the End of the World. Never once did I hear him tell of the Love of God, and maybe it was the terrible things he envisaged that kept the men silent about this. In all the years this old man preached here in the open air, not once was he molested. His audience was uncouth, rough and for the most part uneducated, yet there was respect for a fellow man who lived and preached what he believed to be true.

By today's standards I suppose one would have said we had religion rammed down our throats. I still remember the beautiful hymns we sang in Sunday School, and to my uneducated mind these were true. For instance, we had one hymn which went 'There's a home for little children, above the bright blue sky', and I really believed there was a home up in the sky and dreamed of going there. Another line went 'There's a crown for little children'. I felt certain one day I should wear a crown. The sky to me was a magic place where I should go one day. Perhaps it's as well we did have these fantasies, for it certainly took us in imagination to a better land than the one in which we lived.

CHAPTER ELEVEN

THE HALFWIT BOY

Living quite near to us was a halfwit. He could neither read nor write. He suffered from epileptic fits and he had never had any schooling of any sort. To my way of thinking he was a complete idiot. He played in the street all day long and he was subjected to all kinds of baiting and cruelty by the other children. My mother saw this, and would often invite him in to have a warm. She was the kind of person who could win the confidence of a boy such as he. He was happy and relaxed while he sat with her. She always chose a time to invite him in when the other children were out, thus making him feel she was his friend.

One day my mother left him alone in the kitchen while she made the beds. He found all the old newspapers and put them on the fire. My mother, hearing the roaring of the flames, came to investigate the cause. The boy (Willie) jumped up saying he did not feel well. He raced home and promptly had a fit. My poor mother was left to deal with the fire which she could not put out. Eventually the fire engine was called. It came, horses running and bells ringing, to our house to deal with the fire. The chimney reached six storeys high to the top of the tenements where we lived. Out of the pot belched thick black smoke intermixed with flames. All the encrusted soot up the chimney was alight. The firemen raced to the roof on top of the tenements, taking their hoses with them. They then proceeded to squirt the hoses down the chimney in an effort to put out the fire. The water came pouring down into the kitchen, making everything sooty and wet. My mother was severely reprimanded by the Fire Brigade Chief, who said that if it happened again she would be fined £5. It took us hours to clean up the mess.

Mother did not hold anything against Willie, for she knew he was not right in his mind, but I'm afraid that was the end of her hospitality to Willie, not because of the fire he had caused but for fear of it happening again. The threat of a £5 fine was deterrent enough, for in those days that was indeed a vast amount. Poor Willie came to my mother many times afterwards and could never understand why he was never invited in again.

CHAPTER TWELVE

MY SATURDAY JOBS

As far back as I remember I had a Saturday-morning job. My Mother had a tubercular knee and was unable to kneel. Each week the kitchen and bedroom floors must be scrubbed, and as I was the eldest girl this was my job.

First a galvanised bucket would be filled with hot water and soda. Then a very large hessian apron was fastened round me. It reached to my feet and was meant to prevent me from getting wet. Giving me the bucket, a brush, a floor-cloth, and a bar of 'Lifebuoy' soap, Mother would tell me to start on the bedrooms.

The bedroom we children slept in was small and contained three beds and a few items of furniture. The floor was covered with a cheap floor covering. To clean and scrub this floor was a tactical manoeuvre on my part. I could not move the beds – there was no room. The beds were low, near the floor. If I went flat on the floor and pulled myself along with the wet floor-cloth in my hands, I could just manage to wash the floor underneath them. To scrub the floor I had to slide out backwards, rub soap on to the scrubbing brush and slide back with it again. When that was done, I had to slide out to get the floor-cloth from the bucket and then slide in again to wipe up the water. As my hands were inexperienced in the art of wringing out a floor-cloth, I'm afraid I left the floor very wet. Mother saw this and gave me a dry floor-cloth to dry it with. I had to repeat the performance all over again, until the whole room was finished.

After the bedrooms came the kitchen. The table was scrubbed first, then the seats of the chairs and stools. Only my father's chair was not scrubbed – why I do not know, for it was never polished either. Indeed, I do not remember polish ever being used in my home; there was nothing to polish. The cooker top was the next thing to be cleaned. It was black iron and used to be so encrusted with grease that I had to use a knife to scrape it off. After this came the grate and fireplace, which was cleaned with blacklead until it shone. The hearth was then whitened with hearth-stone, and the fender and fire-irons cleaned with emery paper. This all made a great deal of dust and mess. The last thing to be cleaned was the kitchen floor. No one was allowed in while this was being done, for fear of leaving footmarks behind. In the kitchen I could kneel to do it. My mother instructed me to scrub each piece of floor as far as my arms would stretch, wipe that dry and then move on to the next part. When the floor was completely finished, newspapers were spread over it to help to keep it clean. I need not tell you my knees were sore and tender by the time I had finished the floors.

Window-cleaning was also part of my training. Windows got very dirty and needed to be cleaned each week. The window in my mother's room was the worst. It faced the street, and in front of it were high iron railings with sharp spikes on top. To clean the outside was quite a performance. First, I collected a bucket of cold water and three newspapers. Window-leathers were not used. I climbed out of the window and put one foot on the window-sill and one between the iron spikes of the railings so that I was standing feet astride sideways. I dread to think what could have happened had I fallen, for I could so easily have been impaled on one of the spikes, but I never thought of this at the time. The first newspaper was wetted and used to remove the dirt. The second was for washing the window when most of the dirt was removed. The third was for polishing. If you have never tried it and cannot afford a window-leather, then do as we did and improvise; for, as my mother always told me, 'Where there's a will there's a way.'

These Saturday jobs took up the whole of the morning. There was no thought of payment or reward. They were jobs allocated to me and I accepted them without question.

CHAPTER THIRTEEN

TO HELP A TIGHT BUDGET

At a certain church in East London if you went to Sunday School in the afternoon, you were invited to stay to tea. That meant you were then there for the evening service. The people who stayed to make and serve the tea were church workers and

Sunday School teachers. My sister Kathleen and I were often sent by our parents to this Sunday School, where we stayed on for tea and evening service. We thought this was very boring and often asked my parents if we needed to go, but we always received the same answer: 'If you don't go, you will get no left-overs.' You see, when the service finished in the evening, we were always given all that was left over from tea. There were sandwiches, scones and cake enough to fill a large bag. When we got home they were put away to be eaten on Monday, thus helping out my mother's tight budget.

Another way of saving a little was to go to market on Saturday night just before closing time. The meat traders would sell off the meat cheap in an effort to get rid of it. The men stood shouting to passers-by, holding up joints of meat and reducing it until, as they said, they were almost giving it away. Crowds of East-Enders would make a special journey to buy this cheap meat, for all were in the same boat and everybody had to watch their pennies.

I remember that at a certain baker's shop, which was half-an-hour's walk from home, a loaf of bread was a halfpenny cheaper than at other bakers. Each day, before going to school in the afternoon, I was given the money to buy two loaves, thus making a saving of one penny. Having nowhere to put the money while I was at school, I kept it in my boot, knowing it was safe. (This, as you may guess, was most uncomfortable, but at least the money could not be lost.) I would walk to and from the baker's. Before going into the shop I had to take off my boot in order to get the precious money out. I often wondered if there *was* a saving really, for I think I must have worn out more than one pennyworth of boot-leather during the journey.

CHAPTER FOURTEEN

AN ASSORTMENT OF CLOTHING

You might like to know the way we used to be dressed when I was a young girl. I wore a flannel vest with short sleeves which slipped over the head and had no fasteners. Then came a calico chemise, and over this went what my mother called 'stays', a strip of flannel about eight inches wide fitted round my body and fastened with buttons and buttonholes. Two straps over my shoulder kept it from slipping. On the bottom edge of the stays were six buttons – two at the back and two either side at the front. They were for fastening my knickers on to. The knickers were made with a waistband that fitted round my waist, and on this were the buttonholes to take the buttons on the stays. The back of the knickers had a flap which opened or shut as required. When shut, this was attached to the stays. The knickers were made in what was known as 'fleecy-lined' material. They were grey in colour, reached to the knees and were very cumbersome and awkward, especially if you were in a hurry, for small fingers found it very hard to manipulate buttons at the back side. Many a time we left them undone, not caring if the flap could be seen as we ran along.

Next came a flannelette petticoat with a draw-string through the neck, and then a dress, or whatever else was to hand. I remember my mother once buying an alpaca coat from a jumble sale. It was navy and blue and did up from the neck to hem with about eight buttons. Mother tried it on me and it fitted. She turned it back to front so that I wore it as a dress with the buttons down the back. I wore this many weeks for school and no one questioned its original purpose, for all children were dressed in an assortment of clothes and not one of us derided the other.

My brothers were dressed in flannel vests with Oxford shirts over them. They wore no underpants. Their breeches came to below the knee, where they were fixed into a band which buttoned with two buttons. They each wore a celluloid Eton collar and a tie if one was available. Their socks came just above the band of their breeches so that they were held in place by them. They wore thick heavy boots fitted with studs, tips and Blakeys. Needless to say, these were lovely for sliding along on the pavements. The uppers usually wore out before the soles. In winter they also wore long-sleeved jerseys; the following summer they wore the same jerseys, with the sleeves cut short as these had worn out by then. They did not have overcoats, which were for the better off. Instead, when it was very cold the short-sleeved old jerseys were put under the top jersey for extra warmth. No one wore Wellington boots. These do not appear to have been invented then; if they were, we never saw them. Very few children wore gloves. Some mothers made muffs for their girls, but the majority used cut-down socks to keep small hands warm.

Most girls had a pinafore to wear for Sunday or special events. These pinafores were grand affairs, made of white calico. Frills of broderie anglaise ran round the bottom, while each arm-band had a frill too. The pinafore was usually made with a square yolk in which the gathered material was set. When they had been washed, starched and had their frills goffered, they seemed to us children the height of fashion and we loved wearing them.

Very small children were often sewn up in cotton wool. At the onset of winter a large piece was placed at the back and front and sewn up on the shoulders and sides. The child had to keep it on until the spring came. Each day a piece would be pulled off until all the cotton wool was away from the body. Of course, the child was not given a bath while the cotton wool was worn, and by the time the last piece was off he was very smelly and the cotton wool was black.

For school in winter we wore what we called 'pudding hats',

so called simply because they were shaped like pudding basins. Sometimes they were as tall as eight inches from brim to crown and were finished off with a bobble or tassel.

In the summer months we wore no hat for school, but for Sunday – especially in summer – a large, fancy straw hat was a must. These were beautifully made and trimmed with ribbon or flowers. With our hair hanging loose beneath them we felt wonderful. These hats were put away and preserved from one year to another. If, like my mother, you knew the right place to go to, these beautiful hats could be bought for 1s 11d. The street market in Bermondsey Street, Tower Bridge, was the best place for a bargain; at least, this was my mother's opinion. This was in South London, but it was well worth the long walk from the East End to obtain such bargains.

One year my mother went to Bermondsey Street market and bought my sister and me a dress each. It was the only dress I can ever remember having new. It was bright mauve, and I hated it. It had a high neck with a lace yolk. The bodice was tight and fitted into a full skirt which reached my calves. The sleeves were long and ended in a band at the wrist. The material was shiny and thick. Each Sunday we were obliged to wear them. Then they were carefully put away until the next week. Even taking into account all the makeshift clothes I wore during my childhood, this dress was the only one I disliked wearing. I felt conspicuous and flashy in it and was glad when Monday came so that I could forget it for a week. My mother could not understand why I disliked it so much for she thought I looked lovely in it. Kathleen, being younger, had no thoughts about it all and wore hers without question.

Robert, my eldest brother, went to the Boys School. To me, as a child, this was a frightening place to pass. Boys from every type of home attended there. I had to pass it to get to my own school, and the boys would wait for the girls to come by, then jump out and pull our hair-ribbons and tug at the plaits, chanting, 'Soap, pull the rope.' Before we approached the school we would put our hair inside our overcoats or, in summer, hold it in front of us and chase by the school as fast as we were able. The boys were a mixed lot, some clean, some scruffy and dirty. In an effort to encourage the pupils to take more pride in their appearance, one master offered a weekly prize of a penny to the boy with the cleanest boots, the tidiest hair and the cleanest collar. Once Robert won the penny. There was not a prouder boy in all the East End on that day.

CHAPTER FIFTEEN

DENTISTS AND DOCTORS

We had no dentist when I went to school. We were never bought a toothbrush and we never cleaned our teeth. I remember once having toothache. My mother sent me to the doctor, who promptly sat me in a chair and told me to open my mouth. He said I must have two teeth extracted, obtained what to my frightened gaze appeared to be a pair of pincers, and then, without further ado, pulled the two offending teeth out. No injection, no gas, no freezing of the gums. I can still feel the agony of those few minutes. I thought my head would fall off so hard did he pull, but I would not cry, much as I wanted to, for I dreaded being called a cry-baby. I did have one consolation, however: the doctor told me I was very brave. But it was a long time before that painful incident was forgotten.

Today one has only to feel poorly or in need of a doctor and a telephone call will bring him to your home, or a visit to the surgery will set your mind at rest. You are examined and advised and given treatment. It was not so when I was young. If you were too ill to visit your doctor, you had to send and ask him to call. No doctor we knew had a car – he either rode a bicycle or walked. When he came he carried his black bag with him. We children were convinced he kept new babies in it. His charge for a visit was 3s 6d and this included your medicine. If you went to the surgery, the charge was 2s 6d.

Our doctor's surgery in Stepney was a dark, converted shop with wooden forms running round three sides of it. At one side was a shop counter, half of which was shielded from view by a dark curtain. On shelves over the counter were large bottles of coloured liquid. You waited your turn to see the doctor, taking care to note who was there before you and who came after you. Behind the curtain was a small room where you went when it was your turn. You were given no prescription because the doctor made up your medicine in the surgery behind the dark curtain. We were never given tablets; the medicine was always dispensed as a mixture which, in many cases, was so horrible that it ended up by being poured down the sink.

If you needed hospital treatment, you were given a letter to take to the hospital. The London Hospital in Whitechapel Road was usually the one chosen. You had to present yourself there before nine in the morning. If you arrived later, you were turned away. You were sent to whatever department was necessary and waited on wooden benches until you could be seen by the doctor. Sometimes we sat a whole morning before being attended to. Children were not allowed to run about and no one might talk above a whisper.

The nursing sisters were most formidable. They wore long, blue-striped dresses with long sleeves and stiff cuffs, and a long nurse's apron covered the dress. On their heads they wore a white starched-and-goffered cap. The only thing they ever said was, 'Next, please.'

The hospital was usually crowded with out-patients who, after having waited hours to see a doctor, would be in and out in about five minutes. If medicine was prescribed, then you had to go to the hospital dispensary, where large queues were waiting patiently. Sometimes one would wait an hour or more before being given the prescription. Altogether this was an exhausting business, taking up most of the day.

I remember being sent with Kathleen to the London Hospital, since Mother was unable to take her. Kathleen had what turned out to be a mastoid. She was in great pain and crying pitifully. I carried her all the way from home to the hospital in Whitechapel Road. On arriving we saw the porter who told us where to go. We had the usual long wait, and by the time the doctor saw Kathleen she was in a very bad way. I was told she needed to be kept in hospital but that no beds were available, and I must therefore take her to the local infirmary. By this time it was pouring with rain. I saw the porter again and asked him what I could do. (There was no hospital transport service at this time.) He kindly gave me a large newspaper in which I wrapped Kathleen. We struggled out into the Whitechapel Road to catch a tram to Aldgate. There we alighted and caught another tram which took us as far as London Docks. I carried Kathleen the rest of the way home. She was still wrapped in the newspaper, which by now was soaking wet. Mother was frantic with worry. We hurriedly put Kathleen in a pushchair and took her to our local infirmary, half-an-hours walk away. She was admitted at once and detained for about six weeks.

Looking back at this gross neglect of a sick child in the care of a child not much older, I shudder to think what could have happened on that dreadful journey. Can you imagine the outcry such treatment would evoke today? My sister did recover, but not, I feel, due to any treatment she received at the London Hospital.

On another occasion Mother, who had been ill for a long time with stomach pains, visited the hospital, where she was examined and told she was constipated. She was given an opening medicine and told to come again in a fortnight. Not being satisfied with the diagnosis, she visited Guy's Hospital, which is by London Bridge. There it was discovered that she had cancer which, some painful years later, caused her death.

These incidents, and many others, I think occurred not so much through neglect but because the East End at that time was so heavily populated. With living conditions so bad and wages so low, people did not attend a doctor simply because they could not afford it. Thus the disease or trouble was usually in an advanced stage before treatment was sought.

CHAPTER SIXTEEN

SCHOOL

I should like to describe my school, as I remember it. It was in a narrow street opposite a soap factory and surrounded on three sides by high tenement buildings, and the playground was between the backs of these. Mothers could look out to see the children playing. The school looked as though it had been a wealthy gentleman's house in days gone by. Fancy iron railings ran in front of a small courtyard. The building was two storeys high with an attic above where the caretaker lived. There was a window on either side of the double front door through which you entered into the small hall. Against one wall were large hot-water pipes; opposite was the door of the teachers' room.

At the end of the hall was the infants' school, which took in both boys and girls. There were three classes: first, second and babies. Children were accepted in special circumstances at the age of two-and-a-half. If the mother had a large family or another baby was expected, then the child went to school. These children were not trained and many poor mites had to be cleaned up by the teacher. If the child had an elder sister in the school, then she would be called to clean up the child. Sometimes these babies were so tired by lunch-time that they fell asleep where they sat, much to the relief of the long-suffering teacher, I expect.

At the other end of the passage were the cloakroom and a washroom in which were a few basins with cold-water taps over them. A door led from the washroom to the playground. The playground was small, and at one end it was covered by a glass roof; we played there when it rained. At the end of the part with the glass roof were half-a-dozen toilets, which were always frozen up in winter. The playground was a playground, and nothing more. There were no outdoor games played there other than those we invented. We played 'touch' and skipping and we chased around pretending to be bus-horses.

The girls' school was upstairs. The stairs were very wide and at the top was another cloakroom with wash-basins. Through the double doors were four classrooms: one of medium size at one end; a large room in the middle, which may have been meant for use as a hall, but which was divided down the centre with screens, making it into two classrooms; and at the other end another classroom of medium size. If you were in one of the classrooms where the screens were, it was very difficult to concentrate, as you found yourself listening to what was going on in the class at the other side of the screen. When the whole school assembled, the screens were taken away – which is what makes me think it must have been a hall at some previous time.

If you were in the end classroom and wished to be excused, then you had to walk through the two classes in the hall and through the door which led to the stairs, then down the stairs out into the playground. By this time you either had an accident or things were becoming extremely urgent!

Throughout my years at that school, I always kept to the same classroom, teacher and desk. The room held thirty-six desks; with two girls at each desk, seventy-two girls must have been in the one class. The desks did not open and the seats were attached. Each had an inkwell at either end, filled each day by the ink monitor. We were each given a pen with a nib which had to last a week. Books, too, were given out for each subject and collected and put in a cupboard when the lesson finished. We learned spelling, writing, reading, history, geography, arithmetic and nature study. My one and only prize while at school was for nature study. No one was more surprised than I when I received this prize. I still remember the name of the book. It was *Captain Curly's Boy*. Each year we had a pot-plant competition. Each child who wished could have a geranium or a fuchsia. I always took a fuchsia. The delicate flower of it always delighted me and I longed to win the prize. Alas, I am afraid I always killed it with kindness. Long before it was time to return it each year, it was dead.

We would drone our tables out loud until we knew them by heart, and to this day, if I cannot remember six fives, or seven nines, I repeat the table through until I come to it. The tables were lessons never forgotten. My teacher was Mrs Hamlyn. She was tall, thin and terrifying. If we misbehaved she would bring us out to the front of the class, stand behind us, fold our arms over our chest, and lean over us. Then pushing our sleeves up, she slapped us as hard as she could until our arms burned with the sting. We had a punishment book, kept by the Governess (Headmistress). If you were really naughty, you were sent to the Governess for the cane and to have your name put in red ink in the punishment book. This went against you when you left school, as each of us was given our 'character' (reference) when we left school. Without a good 'character' you could not get a job, as it was always asked for when applying for one. I still have my 'character'. It is one of my treasures, of which I am rather proud.

My Governess – Miss Meikle – was quite old and always dressed in black. She wore a tight bodice with long, tight sleeves drawn into a band at the wrist, and a long, very full skirt which just showed the toes of her black boots. I think she quite liked me, maybe because she had known my mother. Children have a way of knowing who approves or who disapproves. Anyway, I always felt happy in her presence. (I feel I have rambled a bit, but I put these thoughts down as they come to me, for maybe in five minutes' time I shall have forgotten them.)

Back to my classroom. In winter there was a very large coal fire lit before we came into class. In front of it was a large, iron fire-guard. The fire was lovely to look at but didn't seem to warm the classroom. My seat at the back of the class was always cold. I had so many chilblains on my fingers that I sometimes could not hold the pen. Not being able to afford gloves for us, my mother sewed up the legs of worn-out socks and threaded them through with elastic to keep them on. This was quite all right for going to school, but one cannot write with sewn-up socks on one's hands; and so, once at school, I had to go cold.

Most of us girls were very poorly shod, some coming to school with no boots or stockings at all. Those of us who did have them were lucky. Even so, most boots were made with cardboard soles which wore out very quickly, especially in wet weather.

Nobody carried a handkerchief. Pieces of rag did in most cases, but where these were not available sleeves came in most useful. My mother always sewed the hems of her pieces of rag, and mine was always pinned on to my dress to stop me losing it.

Our teachers must have been heroines, for we were for the most part an ignorant and uncouth lot. They persevered, nevertheless, and, much to their credit, turned out some very good girls, who went on to sit for scholarships and, in quite a few cases, made good and were a credit to the school.

We had no homework, therefore no satchels were needed. We had no school milk and no school dinners. If a child was very poor, she could apply for a dinner ticket which entitled her to a free dinner at a coffee-shop. Not many applied for dinner tickets, for even the poor of the community were proud. The children went home for dinner, sometimes to a couple of slices of bread, cut thick to fill them up.

In school we were not allowed to walk about as children do today, and we were not permitted to talk or ask questions. If you disobeyed, you sat with your hands on your head until told to take them off.

I do not think I have mentioned singing. I loved this. Our music and singing teacher was Mrs Leutchford and she taught us many songs. Some come to my mind still: 'The Cuckoo', 'The Ash Grove', 'Now is the Month of Maying', and the hymn 'Through the Day Thy Love has Spared Us'. When I am alone, I find myself singing one or the other and I am there again, singing my heart out, hoping Mrs Leutchford will hear my voice and choose me as a soloist. She never appeared to hear me, although she would come and listen as we sang. I suppose my voice just wasn't good enough.

I believe I have forgotten needlework. We were taught hemming, sew and fell, top-sewing and gathering. Pieces of material were given to each girl and we would have to gather the material in, then stroke the gathers until they all were in a perfectly straight line. I could never see the sense of this, and as we never got any further than the piece of material I'm afraid I never tried very hard. We had no sewing-machines and were never encouraged to make a garment, and so there seemed to be a general dislike of the subject.

As we grew older, we were sent for one half-day a week to a central school for a course of either housewifery, laundry or cooking. We could not choose the course, it was chosen for us. At the laundry we were taught how to wash clothes, iron with a flat iron, goffer with a goffering iron, to starch and to smooth with a smoothing iron. All these processes are now things of the past, and I doubt very much if the young will have any idea of what I am talking about. If we did the housewifery course, we were taught to sweep, dust, polish, make beds and bath a life-size doll. We had great fun on this course, for it was held in a house set aside for the purpose, and with only one teacher in charge we were quick to take advantage when she went to inspect some other part of the house. We jumped on the bed, threw pillows, drowned the doll and swept dirt under the mats. This was the highlight of the week, the one lesson that we never minded going to.

I do not remember our ever having an Open Day; nor was there any Parent–Teacher Association. Parents were not consulted except in the case where a girl was found to have vermin on her. The school nurse came to inspect our heads regularly. We were marched a few at a time into the teachers' room;

there the nurse looked through our hair, using a comb which she dipped in a bowl of carbolic. If your hair was found to contain nits, then you were given a card to take home. If the head had vermin, then you were given a card which warned that if this was not clean by the nurse's next visit you would be sent to the cleansing station, where all your hair was cut very short. This was a disgrace, for all who saw you with your hair cut this way knew you were dirty, and shamed you until the hair grew long again. Many a girl suffered in this way; no one who has not experienced it can understand the misery this practice entailed.

In my school there was no provision for accidents or illness. I remember once swallowing a pin and nearly choking, as it had lodged in my throat. I choked and spluttered so much that I interrupted the lesson. My teacher was told by another girl what had happened. She was nonplussed, as was the Governess. Not knowing what to do they sent me home, still with the pin lodged in my throat. Another girl was sent with me. Luckily, my mother was in when we reached home. She promptly put her fingers in my mouth, making me vomit. Needless to say the pin dislodged itself, but not without scratching my throat. This done, Mother sent me back to school again so that I did not miss my lesson.

Apart from *Paradise Lost*, *Paradise Regained* and *The Bible*, we had no books in our home. From a very early age I wanted to read. I tried *Paradise Lost* and *Paradise Regained*, but they were far beyond my understanding.

Each year for my Sunday School Prize I would ask for a book. This started me on a small collection of books by Dickens, which I read over and over again. Of those I had, I loved *Oliver Twist* best of all. I went through all Oliver's trials with him. I cried over him and loved him, for in those early days we lived in such conditions and it was easy for me to identify myself with him. I knew the threat of the workhouse, the threat of prison and bread-and-water. If we misbehaved, all these threats were held against us and we were fearful of being sent there. I also acquired *Uncle Tom's Cabin*. This was about the slave trade in America. I loved Uncle Tom and his family, and I adored Topsy, who said, 'I never had no father or mother, I 'spect I growed.' Those books and others, all with a moral, were my only reading with the exception of the history and geography books at school, which I hated. I do not remember ever having an interesting story-book to read at school. William, my brother, had *Hans Andersen's Fairy Tales* as a prize and he let me read these. Then I was carried away in a world of fantasy and make-believe. I treasured these books for many years, only to lose them in the bombing during World War Two.

When I was older I attended the central school full time. It was situated in the Jewish quarter in Stepney. On Fridays we had what was called 'double session'. Usually we had two hours for lunch break, but on Fridays we had only an hour. On all other days we left school at four o'clock but on Friday we left at two-thirty. This enabled the Jewish children among us to get home, have a meal and prepare for their Sabbath, which started at sunset on Friday evening and spread over Saturday. On my way home from school I used to make myself a nice bit of sweet-money, for if I walked slowly along, Jewish women would ask me to light their gas, or put a match to their fire or bank it up with coal. In fact any small job that needed to be done, I did. If a Christian could not be found, then the job went undone, for the Jews in that area observed their religious rites most strictly. The table was laid with a clean, white cloth upon which stood candles especially kept for the Sabbath. I was paid one halfpenny for each job done and welcomed the chance to earn some sweet-money so easily.

CHAPTER SEVENTEEN

PADDLE STEAMERS

During the summer season a host of paddle steamers taking people on pleasure trips could be seen going down the Thames. One could stand and watch the busy scene and never tire of looking. I would go as far as to say that the river then was something like the roads of today, only safer. Nothing ever seemed to stand still.

It is one of my regrets that I did not gather some knowledge from the people I know who worked on the paddle steamers before 1914, but I do know enough to record a few details of these fine old boats. The Yarmouth and Clacton boats sailed from Fresh Wharf and Nicolsons Wharf, below London Bridge. They were the 'Belle Steamers', *Yarmouth Belle*, *Walton Belle*, and *Southend Belle*. I think there were others in the fleet, but cannot recall them. The General Steam Navigation Co ran the 'Eagle Steamers', among which were *Eagle* and *Golden Eagle*. After the First World War in the 1920's they had built the *Royal Eagle*, and in 1925 *Crested Eagle*. The *Crested Eagle* had a telescopic funnel to enable her to pass under London Bridge to Old Swan Pier close by. During the 1930's General Steam alone sailed steamers from London to Southend, Ramsgate, Margate, Yarmouth and Clacton, and also to Boulogne. Theirs were the new screw steamers, *Royal Daffodil*, *Royal Sovereign*, *Royal Primrose* and *Kingfisher*.

Before the First World War and in competition with the Belle Steamers and the Eagles, the New Palace Steam Co had paddle steamers, *Royal Sovereign* and *Koh-i-Nur*. Both had telescopic funnels and sailed from Old Swan and All Hallows Piers, to Southend, Ramsgate and Margate. They also had *La Margarette* which sailed from Tilbury to Boulogne. There is a model of *Royal Sovereign* in the Maritime Museum at Greenwich and I believe *Koh-i-Nur* is in the Science Museum at South Kensington.

During the 1914–18 War many of these ships were in service as hospital ships. When the war ended a Company was formed in 1919. They sailed the old *Royal Sovereign* alone from Old Swan Pier to Southend, Ramsgate and Margate. The skipper was one Captain Kelly. The *Koh-i-Nur* and *La Margarette* never came back to the Thames. I believe *Koh-i-Nur* went to Bristol and *La Margarette* sailed somewhere off the East Coast. *Royal Sovereign* was sold to a Dutch Company and was eventually broken up. Somewhere in Kent in a back garden is one of her paddle boxes, and some of her cabin fittings are preserved in one of the rooms in the house.

In 1920 some of the Belle Steamers came back into service and the General Steam Co sailed *Eagle* and *Golden Eagle*. There used to be some exciting races between *Golden Eagle* and *Royal Sovereign* to get to Southend first. They were a well-matched pair and often steamed neck-and-neck for miles. The first one to get to Southend would of course be first to get to the other piers too, and first home at night.

These boats had sweet shops, licensed bars, barber's shops and excellent restaurants where sumptuous meals were served. I think that their passing is a sad loss. Chasing about in cars and coaches is not one tenth the pleasure of a cruise on a paddle steamer!

CHAPTER EIGHTEEN

CONDITIONS

It is surprising to me, when I think back on the poverty which existed in those far-off days, the way people accepted it. Most were content with their lot and made no effort to better themselves. I think religion played a great part in this. I remember a hymn we used to sing, which will give you some idea of its teaching. It goes:

> The rich man in his castle,
> The poor man at his gate,
> He made them high or lowly
> And ordered their estate.

Could it be that the estate of rich and poor was ordered by some divine being? It is inconceivable that today's generation would believe such a teaching. Women and girls working on sewing-machines in the dark, damp basements of old houses doing sweated labour in bad conditions and for poor wages; girls who, as they grew up pretty and attractive, went to the West End to sell themselves because they found this was the only way to make money: could these things have been ordered as our 'estate'? I think not. Poor education, bad conditions, want and poverty; these were the lot of the majority and were responsible for most of the ills of that generation. My father once summed up his life in a nutshell: 'Eat, drink, sleep and work – this is my life.' And in his case, I can only agree.

The conditions and the constant struggle to make ends meet made a woman lose her interest in herself and her looks. As they grew older, many people lost their teeth. They went toothless, not knowing or caring what they looked like. A woman was considered to be old at fifty. Today, one cannot tell if a woman is twenty-five or fifty-five, so great now is the art of make-up. A woman can happily have a career and be confident knowing she can apply all the modern aids to keep her beautiful. For it is the hope of every woman to remain young and attractive. Not so with the women when I was a child. Most married and had large families. Many women wore a man's cap, kept on by means of a long hatpin. The point sometimes stuck out so far that if you got too near you were in danger of being caught by it. Skirts reached almost to the ground, and when it rained it became so muddy that the women would either hold them up off the ground or insert a large safety-pin through a tuck made to hold the hem out of the mud.

Very few women wore make-up and the occasional one who did was considered by the rest to be 'no good'. I do not remember ever seeing a woman smoke when I was a child. As I grew older and this practice started, there was a great wagging of tongues and pointing of fingers, for women smokers too were considered to be on the downward path. Although this was a poor working-class community, people had a great sense of values regarding moral behaviour. Each woman kept to her own man, and would not have dreamed of doing otherwise. Sometimes the men were very cruel to their women, especially when in drink. I have heard many a woman screaming and shouting as a drunken man gave her a good hiding. The following day she would emerge with black eyes and swollen face, yet would not utter a word against her husband – and woe-betide anyone who did! Not a word would she have against him.

One of the saddest things I remember was to see women drunk, although it happened quite often. To see a drunken man was bad enough, but to see a woman so really troubled me. One incident in particular stands out in my mind: a woman who was so drunk she stood in the middle of the road, offering to fight anyone who would take her on. She took off her clothes, cursing and shouting, until she had nothing on, to the great amusement of the crowd who had gathered around. Finally the police came and carted her away to the police station, where I presume she slept it off. There were methylated spirit drinkers, too, and most of these were women. Methylated spirit was quite cheap and could be drunk in the privacy of one's home. These women became so addicted they nearly always died at an early age.

I hope I do not give the impression that all the women were bad; indeed the majority were clean, patient and hardworking, bringing up families under the worst kinds of conditions. They cleaned their windows each week, and their curtains were taken down and washed every fortnight. They got so black that you soaked them in salted water before you washed them. When this water was poured away it was as black as soot. The air was full of smoke and grime from many factories and ships, and from the coal fires which everyone used, but each fortnight those curtains went up clean.

Then there were the doorsteps. Each front door had a wooden doorstep, which was scrubbed white each morning. The pavement outside the house was swept and then the woman of the house, kneeling down with a bucket of hot water and some whitening, proceeded to wash the pavement immediately in front of her door, making a half-circle which she would afterwards whiten with the whitening. Thus each house you passed had its half-circle of white pavement and its white-scrubbed doorstep. When the front door opened, in many cases one would see laced curtains draped just half-way down the passage – or hall, as it is now called. This looked nice, and also prevented people seeing into the room beyond, which in nearly every case was the living-room-cum-everything. No matter how poor or how little a family had, this outward appearance had to be kept up at all costs.

CHAPTER NINETEEN

MILK, BREAD, GROCERIES AND SMELLS

Looking back over the years, I see a great change in people's habits. Today one orders one's milk. It is delivered in sealed bottles which have been sterilised. The milk is fresh and one can enjoy drinking it. When I was a little girl, the milkman came round the streets calling 'Milko'. If you were a regular buyer, he would pour your pint or half-pint into a galvanised can that had a handle, and hang it on your door-knob. If you wanted milk only occasionally, then you went out with your milk jug. The milkman's barrow held a churn containing the milk, and at the front of the churn was a tap. The milkman had two galvanised measures, a pint and a half-pint, and each had a bent handle. When not in use the handle fitted inside the top of the churn. If you only wanted a penny-worth, then the milkman would judge how much you should have. He wore a blue-and-white-striped apron over his trousers and usually smelled awful. I suppose milk must have splashed on to his clothes — and nothing smells worse than stale milk.

Most people in our community drank very little of this milk, preferring to use sweetened, condensed, skimmed milk which was cheaper and did not go bad, as did the cows' milk. We also had a small milk-shop quite near to us where you could take your jug and buy the milk you needed. This was a very clean shop, kept by a Welshman and his wife. They also sold butter and biscuits. The counter was of white marble and on it stood a large china container full of milk. The measures hung inside it and floated about on top of the milk. A muslin cloth covered it, but this did not prevent flies entering and falling in. (In those days flies were a serious pest. There were no sprays such as we have today, and people bought fly-papers in an effort to get rid of them. These were rolls of sticky paper which were unrolled and hung up. The flies caught themselves on it and were held fast by the glue. Sometimes a paper would become black with buzzing flies, all trying in vain to get free.) The butter from the milk-shop was not sold in packets as it is to-day. Most people could not afford butter but very occasionally I would be sent out for two ounces. The shopkeeper took off the required amount, weighed it, then patted it into shape with wooden butter-pats which he kept in a basin of water. The butter was always for Mother, who was an invalid. We children nearly always had dripping.

Bread was mostly baked on the premises by small bakers. One of the most pleasureable things I remember was the smell of fresh-baked bread. On Sundays, the baker would open not for the sale of bread but for the convenience of his customers. Sunday joints were prepared, put into baking tins together with potatoes and taken to the baker. He would cook them for you in his oven, charging you twopence for his trouble. At one o'clock a steady stream of people made their way back to collect their Sunday joint, hurrying home again as quickly as possible to enjoy their well-cooked dinner. They were happy days in that close-knit community. The feeling of belonging outclassed everything else. There was poverty, disease, dirt and ignorance, and yet to feel one belonged outweighed all else.

I think now about our grocer. He kept a small, dark shop close by the tenements. He sold everything from bacon to paraffin-oil. He was as clean as could be under the circumstances, and if he had just sold a pint of paraffin and you went in for a rasher of bacon, he would quickly wipe his hands on a piece of rag before cutting off the requested rasher. He had no bacon-cutting machine. It was not surprising that often you would have the flavour of paraffin mixed with you bacon. He sold loose jam (or rather jam-flavoured preserve, which he stocked in seven-pound jars), and he would sell you one penny-worth. When you wanted to buy some, you took a basin which he carefully weighed. Then putting on an extra ounce weight, he weighed your jam straight into the basin. For tea, we often had this on bread without any butter.

Mondays was washing day for everyone, and because there was little time for cooking, this day was 'cold meat day'. So on Mondays one could see children going to the grocer, each with a basin, to buy one pennyworth of mustard pickle. He followed the same procedure when weighing the pickle as he did for jam.

One cannot mention the East End of London without associating it with fish-and-chip shops. To hungry people the smell of these establishments was delightful. Only to stand and smell made one's mouth water. At lunch-time and in the evening these shops were always crowded with people, all shouting their orders. People did not queue in those days. You pushed and shoved in an effort to get served before your neighbour. Most orders were for a halfpenny piece of fish and a halfpennyworth of chips, which were served to you in newspaper. People saved old newspapers to sell to the proprietor for about one penny a bundle. *Nothing* was wasted.

There were pork butchers who sold delicious faggots and pease pudding. When you wanted these you took your jug or basin and, according to how many were in your family, you bought one faggot for each person, plus two pennyworth of pease pudding. (In case you do not know, a faggot is a savoury rissole, square in shape, made from liver, bread and spices.) A generous helping of gravy was included. When times were very hard my mother made faggot stew. Putting the faggots in with potatoes and onion, she stewed them until they disintegrated into the water. When served to us for dinner it made an appetising and nourishing meal.

In most market places there was an eel-and-pie shop. Outside on a stall live eels were displayed in metal containers. They slithered about like snakes and it must have required great skill to handle them, for they were slippery and slimy. People bought eels by the pound. The stallholder grabbed as many as were wanted and weighed them. Then he put each eel on a wooden board and with a sharp knife chopped them into pieces about an inch long. These were taken home and cooked with parsley butter sauce, and those who fancied them considered them a luxury.

The shop sold stewed eels, meat pies and mashed potatoes. On a winter's day, especially after the morning shopping was done, women and children would go there to have their dinner. The shop was warm and had a wonderful smell. Most customers bought two pennyworth of eels and a pennyworth of mash, covered by the liquor in which the eels were cooked. Flavoured with parsley, this dish was considered a feast. For those who could not afford eels, one pennyworth of mash covered with liquor sufficed. Pies were also served, with mash and liquor. On Saturdays I went out with my mother and we often had a meal in an eel-and-pie shop. Nothing was ever enjoyed so much. Special shops like these seem to be things of the past. Only the fish-and-chip shops remain, and even these are now not the homely, friendly places that I knew. The fish-and-chip fryers of those far-off days might have had no knowledge of hygiene, but they certainly knew how to fry fish and chips to perfection.

In the Sunday morning market were hundreds of stalls, all selling goods of every description. The one which stays in the mind is the sarsaparilla wine stall. Sarsaparilla wine, according to the seller, would do you no end of good and put new life into you. It was sold at a few pennies a glass. The taste was very pleasant, and even if you didn't experience a feeling of new life, at least it was a refreshing drink.

Another stall sold apple-fritters, which looked something like ringed doughnuts. The smell of these cooking in the open really made your mouth water, and the men who made and sold these usually did a roaring trade.

Other shops sold sausage and mash. Their windows were full of large containers of sausages, tomatoes, onions and peas, all sizzling and cooking as you watched. The smell was delicious and made our mouths water. I never went into one of these shops but I often went to enjoy the lovely smell!

One also smelt spices from the spice mill, pepper from the pepper factory, boiling jam from the jam factory and biscuits cooking at the biscuit factory. All these, and many others, come back to me as I write. Of course there were the unpleasant smells as well, but these seem to have faded into the background and only the good smells stay clear in my memory.

CHAPTER TWENTY

LOOKING OVER LONDON BRIDGE

If you had walked over Tower Bridge from the City side you would have come to Tooley Street, a gloomy street of tall warehouses, tenement buildings, and railway arches. St. Olaf's School and Church once stood at the beginning of the street, but by the time I was born they had been replaced by wharves and warehouses belonging to Hays Wharves. These extended along the whole of the riverside from Tower Bridge to below London Bridge. Opposite these in Tooley Street stood the tenements.

Further up were the arches above which ran the railway. The arches were used as storehouses, having wooden doors attached to them. Some were open to the public for the sale of fish. As there was no refrigeration these were most unpleasant and smelly. These conditions put me off fish for a very long time. Another arch was used for storing eggs and the smell as you walked by was nauseating. At the end of the arches, you would have seen a flight of stone stairs leading up to London Bridge.

Had you looked over you could have seen Hays Wharf on the south side of the river. This was one of the most famous groups of warehouses on the Thames and to it came ships from all over the world. The first of the tea clippers came here to unload its cargo. The tea was stored in the warehouse and it is said when the tide was high the warehouse was flooded, spoiling the tea. New Fresh Wharf was there, with ships berthed close by. Crane drivers would have been at work on the great cranes, lifting cases of oranges from a Spanish ship and manipulating them into the loopholes to be received by dockers who stored them in the warehouse or loaded them into waiting carts drawn by horses and eventually taken to the markets. You would also have noticed the barges being towed by steamtugs, the hooting of ships, the shouting of men, the noise of the cranes – a thousand-and-one things to watch and listen to as you stood for your free look over the bridge.

As you stood and stared you might have noticed the Sun Tugs, which looked very colourful with their black funnels and wide bright-red band. They were steam-driven, and towed ships and barges up and down river and in and out of the docks. Many were hired by Tate and Lyle, the two sugar refiners. They had a crew of six, Captain, Mate, Deckhand, Engineer, Stoker and Boy. These men worked very long hours, and had to wait for the tide to rise before towing a ship in or our of the dock, or taking it up or down river. Barges need only a shallow depth of water, it was not unusual to see a tug towing four or more barges. There were large and small Sun Tugs, all of them named after the sun. These tugs operated from Tunnel Pier at Wapping. I had a great affection for them for my husband, Reuben, worked on the *Sunfly* for many years. When our children were small we often went to watch the river from Tower Bridge. If we saw a Sun Tug approaching we would wait to see if it was the *Sunfly*. Then, if it was, we would wave as it passed under the bridge, hoping this would be the last job for the day, for we never knew when work would finish. Maybe it would be out all night and tie up early next day, for these men worked with the tide and were never sure when work would finish!

Now I see a great change on the river. Gone are the great docks, gone is the hustle and bustle of fussy little ships. The great clanking cranes are rusting and silent. The small isolated communities who lived and worked on the river are gone. I revisited my part of the river some time ago, and could scarcely recognise it. It was a dead and derelict place. The people were gone, and the place seemed to be filled with the sound of the tramp of men searching for work, of the laughter of the children who once played here, all I suspect now cooped up in high rise flats; for not far off I saw them shutting out the skyline, just as did the high dock walls so many years ago.

CHAPTER TWENTY-ONE

PRIVATE BATHS AND PUBLIC BATHS

Today there are no houses built without a bathroom and an inside toilet: these things are a must. In the days I speak of, not one house in our community had a bath or an inside toilet. The toilet was usually at the bottom of the yard. Some had running water but many were earth closets. Toilet paper was unheard of. I am not saying that it was not in use elsewhere, but it certainly wasn't in our community. Regularly each week sheets of newspaper were cut into squares of appropriate size, threaded through one corner with string and hung up on a nail. They had to serve the purpose. No one washed after using the closet, and I doubt if such action was ever thought about.

Men who had toiled all the week in filthy jobs needed a hot bath, and with nowhere to bath and no privacy it was quite something to manage it without interruption. I remember a man we were acquainted with taking a bath one Sunday afternoon when all his family were home. The father decided to take his bath in the bedroom. The bath was half a wooden beer barrel, complete with bung. He and his wife carried buckets of hot water into the bedroom until the barrel was half full. The bung was at the bottom of the barrel, being removed to empty it. Being large, the father could sit in the barrel only if he let his legs stay outside. He stepped into the barrel and washed as much of himself as he was able. Then he decided to sit down and wash the rest of himself. Alas, he sat on the bung, which came out of the hole. Away ran the water, flooding the bedroom floor and seeping into the tenement below. Mother and children were amazed to see the kitchen door suddenly open as the father, as naked as he was born, rushed in carrying the barrel in front of him to cover his nakedness. Never did I laugh so much as when this story was told to me. I need not tell you it took a long time for the father to live that down. It was a much longer time before he ventured to take another bath. We laughed at a tale such as this, and perhaps it was as well people could laugh at such situations, but I guess the people of today would find it no laughing matter.

One could go to the public baths if one had twopence to spare. The baths were half-an-hour's walk from home. You paid your twopence and were given a towel so stiff it stood on end. The attendant had a key with which she controlled the tap. She doled out your water and left you. It didn't matter if the water was too hot or too cold; you couldn't do anything about it. If the water was too hot, you burned yourself; and if it was too cold, you froze. The attendant would never come back once she had given you your water.

I went once when I was about twelve with Nellie, a friend of mine. We were both given our water. Mine was too hot and Nellie's too cold. The cubicle was open at the top of the wall, and if we shouted we could talk to each other. We could also throw over to each other anything that we wanted. Nellie called to me to say that she had no soap. I had known that soap was not provided and had taken a bar of 'Sunlight' with me. Not having anything to cut it with, but deciding to share it nevertheless, I proceeded to bite it in half. Have you ever tasted 'Sunlight' soap? It was horrible, but I persevered until it was in two pieces. Then I threw one piece over to Nellie. We then decided that as we had paid our twopence, we were going to get our money's worth, and so we began to wash our hair. We both had very long, thick hair. I nearly scalded myself, while poor Nellie nearly froze. In the middle, the attendant came in. She told us that hair washing was not allowed, and gave us five minutes to get out. My hair was full of soap which I couldn't rinse off and Nellie was shivering with the cold, her hair hanging down like wet rats' tails. As soon as the five minutes were up, we were promptly turned out, cold, wet and miserable. That was our first and last visit to the public baths.

Alongside the public baths was the public wash-house where women could go to do their washing, not with washing-machines and driers but with rubbing-boards and soap. Early on most Monday mornings, one could see the women trundling prams piled high with dirty washing, a wooden rubbing-board perched on top. Each woman took a coarse apron with her. They were made from sacks obtained from the warehouses. She wore this in an effort to keep dry while doing the washing. At the wash-house were rows of wooden sinks, and below on the floor a kind of gulley where the spilt water ran. The women leaned on the rubbing-boards and rubbed the washing up and down the boards. If a woman was big at the bust it could be very painful, for the top of the board reached to the bust. Each woman pinned a square of mackintosh to her front in an effort to keep her chest dry, but with so much rubbing up and down the whole morning, they were all usually very wet by the time they had finished. Before she left, each woman had to clean up the mess she had made, and leave the channel clean for the next user. She then loaded the wet washing back into the pram and took it home to dry. It was an exhausting business for, as I mentioned, the wash-house was quite half-an-hour's walk away from home.

CHAPTER TWENTY-TWO

THE PORTRAIT

I do not remember us having a mirror in our house. I have no recollection of ever looking at myself. My mother saw to it that we washed hands, face and neck each day. She did our hair, parting it down the middle from the forehead to the back of the neck and combing half to each side. Taking each half she pulled it straight back as tight as it would go and plaited it so that we had two plaits. When the plaits were three-parts done, she would insert the hair-ribbon into the hair and finish the plait with hair and ribbon. She then tied a knot in it and made the end into a little round knob. The ribbon was tied into a bow with a double knot, making it impossible for us to lose it. When we returned home from school in the afternoon our hair was as tidy as when we had gone in the morning. Looking back I can find nothing attractive in this, yet the art master at a school I attended for a short period asked me if I would sit for him while he painted my portrait. I sat for him many times during dinner breaks. When the portrait was finished he gave me my reward – a used tennis ball, which I was delighted with. He also showed me the portrait. I was most disappointed, having thought I would see a picture of a pretty little girl. All I saw was a girl with her hair scragged back, two large scared-looking eyes and a short turned-up nose. I was disappointed, not believing I could look like that. I suppose the art teacher must have seen something that appealed to him, but what it was I shall never know.

CHAPTER TWENTY-THREE

STREET NAMES

Many of the street names conjured up a picture totally different from that which they presented in fact. I think I must have been a bit of a dreamer, for I saw the outward things with an inward vision. Paradise Row was one such. Can you imagine a more tranquil name? Actually it was a narrow court with houses on three sides. Washing lines stretched across its width. I can only assume that the houses had no backyards, for people and washing alike were here for all to see. Mothers passed the time at their doors, some sitting on their doorsteps with crowds of children playing around. There was nothing to see there but the neighbours and the occasional stranger who came by accident to this place, only to hurry away again, possibly ashamed and embarrassed by what he saw.

I think of Nightingale Lane. The song of the nightingale is a joy to listen to, but I doubt if even a sparrow chirped in that street, a narrow lane running between the high dock-walls. It was dreary and desolate and only the bravest would walk alone there at night, for here and there were dark doorways and narrow gateways leading to the docks. Each time I walked this way when a child, I was convinced that someone was hiding ready to jump out at me, and so I walked in the middle of the road, sometimes running in a panic down that forbidding lane.

Pearl Street: a back street in the heart of dockland with nothing in it but dark, drab little houses and hardworking people whose one aim in life was to keep body and soul together. I doubt very much if anyone there would have known a pearl had they seen one. And in any case, their thoughts and minds were on more mundane things. They were concerned with work, bread and the money with which to make ends meet.

Again I see Arbour Square, containing the chief police station. Here were brought drunks and other petty criminals. The rest of the Square was filled with neat little houses. People did not sit outside these houses, for this place had an air of respectability. The houses were clean and well cared for, and I suspect they may even have had gardens behind them where people might chat over their walls and so did not need to sit on their doorsteps. I am surmising, but even so I very much doubt if any one of them contained an arbour, such as I visualised.

Fashion Street! Does it call to mind fashionable ladies and smart gentlemen? Let me destroy this illusion! It was a short, narrow street of small, dark, boarded-up shops let out as stores for wholesalers and the Jewish tailoring trade. It led into Spitalfields with its beautiful old church, to whose crypt and churchyard came the down-and-outs. In the daytime they occupied all the seats or sat on the grass while at night, and indeed in the daytime too, they slept in the crypt, having nowhere else to go. East Enders knew this churchyard as 'Itchy

Park' and considered it a place to be avoided for, although we were poor, we at least had our pride and none had sunk so low as they who daily gathered there.

Before London was invaded by so many different races and before the narrow streets and high walls were built, many parts were small villages and country places. I can only think that these street names were an inheritance from those cleaner, more tranquil days.

CHAPTER TWENTY-FOUR

PENNY IN THE SLOT, AND PARLOURS

The tenements we lived in were lit by gas. We had three gas jets, one in each room. They were fixed to an arm on the wall about three feet from the ceiling. The kitchen one had an upright mantle fitted to it, fixed from the top and hung suspended on a small forked rod. The mantles were very fragile, and if not covered by a globe would blow off or break if a draught caught them. Two chains hung down from each side of the lamp and by pulling them the light could be controlled. On the ceiling above the light was a large, black ring of soot, for if the gas was not regulated properly it burned the ceiling. Later on, inverted mantles were introduced. These were fixed so that they hung down. They gave a much better light, but were still dangerous if not fitted with a globe. With all the washing and airing hanging around it, it was a wonder there were not more fires than there were.

We had a penny-in-the-slot meter for the gas and when the penny 'ran out' the light would gradually get dimmer. Great was the scramble to find another penny quickly before we were left in darkness. The two jets in the bedrooms had no mantles — just a fan-shaped flame. In our home we seldom used these, Mother seeing us to bed by candle-light and then taking the candle away, leaving us in darkness.

The passage which led to the street doors also had a naked flame and gave a very poor light. I remember being very frightened in winter when it was dark early, as to reach the street door we had to go down the dark passage. At the end of the passage was a flight of dark stairs leading up to the passage above. It was not unusual to find a tramp asleep on the stairs, or one or two children waiting to jump out on you.

Except in the case of the very poorest houses, everyone had a parlour. This was a room, usually in the front, into which visitors were asked. It was usually freezing cold, for it was never used except on very special occasions such as weddings and funerals. Normally it contained a horsehair sofa and four high-backed chairs. At each side of the fireplace was a black arm-chair, also stuffed with horsehair. A table, usually of heavy oak and round or oval in shape, stood in the centre of the room, and in the middle of the table was a coloured-glass centre-piece. A small, high table stood in the window with an aspidistra in a fancy-art pot placed on it. (The lace curtains were drawn back just enough to show the plant and the pot.) In one corner stood a 'what-not' – a piece of furniture used to display ornaments and odds and ends. On each chair was an anti-macassar, usually hand-worked or crocheted. The mantelpiece had a crocheted runner stretching from end to end. These were 'a must'. They were made in macramé and were very intricate. The pattern was usually threaded through with ribbon, and a bow was made in the centre of it. On the mantelpiece usually stood a black-marble clock complete with matching side ornaments. An overmantel of mirror-glass stood against the wall on the mantelpiece, so that everything in the room was reflected. Most parlours had a piano adorned by photographs and ornaments. Pictures in large, gilt frames hung on the walls.

Parlours were indeed the show-places of the poor of my generation, and I always envied those of my friends who boasted such a room. It was something we never had. You may wonder how the furniture and ornaments came to be paid for. Certainly people did not have ready money. They either paid into the loan club or had a tallyman who would deliver the goods and was paid once a week when he called. If by any chance you hadn't the money and decided not to answer the door when he came, then the tallyman took out his anger on the knocker.

Drinking and the tallyman were two of the worst evils of my time, for in many cases people did not seem able to resist either. My father would not allow Mother to be in a club or to have a tallyman. One of his sayings was, 'What we haven't got we'll go without, for if we cannot pay one week, we cannot pay two.' This and other similar sayings have so instilled themselves in my memory that I still find it impossible to bring myself to have anything for which I cannot pay ready money.

CHAPTER TWENTY-FIVE

THE RAG MAN

I am now the proud possessor of two tea-sets, which are displayed in a cabinet for all to see. I suppose I think more highly of my china than do most people because in my young day a best tea-set was unknown in our community. We acquired our cups, saucers and plates from the rag man who came every afternoon with a hand-barrow on which was displayed all manner of earthenware. We heard him calling, 'Rags for china,' as he approached. If Mother was short of a cup, she would sort out any old clothes she had until she had quite a bundle. Then we children would run out and offer them to him. He would give us a thick earthenware cup brightly painted with flowers if he thought the clothes were worth it. In this way, we were kept supplied with the only china we possessed.

The baby always had an enamel mug, known to us as 'the big enamel whacker'. Another mug was kept by the sink, so that we children could have a drink of water whenever this was required. Some families had no cups at all and used jam-jars for drinking purposes. Father had a moustache-mug. When he drank, his moustache was kept dry by resting on a ledge across the top of the cup. I was always fascinated by this cup and I never tired of watching him drink from it. These mugs have long since gone out of fashion.

When a neighbour called, a cup of tea was given as a sign of welcome. Indeed, if she were not offered tea she would feel she was *not* welcome and would not come again. The rag man's cups were used when visitors called. It was the best china we had. I expect if you had gone into more wealthy homes it would have been different, but I can only tell you of the things I remember of the poor of those days.

CHAPTER TWENTY-SIX

A WEEK BY THE SEA

One year we spent a week at Yarmouth. We of course went by paddle steamer. On a certain Saturday in August, buckets and spades were ready, a large black gladstone bag was packed with sandwiches, and my father and Robert carried a wooden trunk between them holding a handle each. We all walked, Father, Mother and us children from Wapping to Fresh Wharf, near London Bridge. My mother, who carried the baby, wore her black sailor-type straw hat and a long full skirt which nearly reached the ground. Around her neck she wore as a scarf a large folded white towel. This was for mopping the baby up if it were sick. My father had bought the tickets for the paddle steamer beforehand and placed them inside the headband of his white straw hat for safe-keeping. To carry them this way saved packing them.

On our arrival at Yarmouth we children were bundled straight to bed. We had been travelling for twelve hours and it had been an exciting and tiring day. My parents had booked cooking and attendance. For the holiday we were all dressed in a bright red jersey, so that however far we wandered our parents could easily pick us out. (One day I had been lost on the beach. My parents were distracted and I was terrified. Hence the bright red jerseys we all wore after that.)

Living in the East End of London we often had winkles for tea. We were very ignorant about living creatures. On going for a walk one day, my brother and I saw a very old pebbled wall, such as you never saw in London. On it were hundreds of winkles (or so we thought). We pulled those winkles off the wall and filled our buckets with them. Here was something for nothing! We ignored the small ones, choosing only the fattest and largest. Anticipating a feast at teatime, we chased back to our landlady and offered them to her. We were astounded when she told us they were snails, not winkles. She forbade us to let them loose in her garden. Very crestfallen, we took them back again and tried to stick them on the wall but they refused to stick so we took them and threw them into the sea. I very much doubt if any of them survived.

It was against the law to undress on the beach. Large wooden huts with wooden wheels stood at the water's edge and in these people undressed, only to dress again before entering the sea to bathe. I remember seeing ladies who donned hats or bonnets and a pair of pantaloons reaching to the ankle. These were covered by a tunic reaching to the knees, with long sleeves which reached the wrist. A pair of boots completed the outfit. None of the body was exposed, it being deemed indecent. The men usually wore a striped one-piece outfit reaching the knees. These had half-sleeves. The bathers stepped from the hut into the sea. As the tide receded, the huts were pulled farther out, so that the bathers would be unobserved. If the beach was stony or shingly a kind of canvas mat was laid down for the bathers to walk on. They usually frisked about, playing in the water and never once did I see a lady get her hat or bonnet wet through immersion in the sea. When I see healthy tanned young people bathing on our beaches today I marvel at the change that has come about since I was a little girl!

I must pay tribute to the Captains of the paddle steamers. It is fitting to speak of these men, for they were inspired with the sense of responsibility entrusted to them. Many had worked their way up from the rank of Able Seamen to that of Captain. Over four hundred thousand passengers were carried on these boats during a season and it is on record that not a single life was lost through any cause over which these men had control.

The steamers never ran on Fridays. This was the day set aside for maintenance. As each ship returned each evening to London, she would tie up for refuelling and watering. The humpers and donkeymen used to work all night carrying buckets of coal out of barges, using a Jacob's ladder, and putting tons of coal on board. By the time they had finished they were blacker than the coal they carried. The men from the water-barges came too, and had to pull the hoses all over the deck as some vessels had seven or eight different tanks, some for boilers and others for catering and drinking. These men certainly knew the meaning of work, for after the waterbarges were emptied they had to go to fill up again. All told there were about 100 to 120 tons of water put on board each steamer every night. The men finished about four or five a.m., and then carried on with the normal day's work. I tell you this as I think the comparison with today's standard is obvious.

The crew of the Paddle Steamers were employed only for the season. They received a very poor remuneration for their services. Most were cockneys living by or near the river. To supplement their meagre wage they thought up some ingenious practices which demonstrated true cockney initiative. They would try them out on the unsuspecting passengers. When a ship reached the more open and windy spaces of the Thames Estuary, a very old battered hat was quietly dropped overboard by one of the crew. At once a cry would be raised by another member of the crew 'Gentleman lorst 'is 'at!' A collection was then made by another member of the crew to help buy a new hat for the non-existent gentleman. A second money-raiser was most cunning. A crew member would casually station himself by a ventilator, and solemnly throw pennies down the shaft, taking care to be wide of the mark. Naturally the men among the passengers would have a go to see if they could do better, with the result that a bucket placed at the bottom of the ventilator shaft soon filled with pennies. These and many other practices helped to swell the crews' wages, and also provided some amusement for crew and passengers alike.

CHAPTER TWENTY-SEVEN

SWINGING ROUND THE LAMP-POST

In the days I write about, every child played in the street as soon as it could walk. We did not possess many toys and so invented our own games, some of which I have already mentioned. One in particular was a great favourite.

The streets were lit by gaslight. The lamp-posts were made of cast iron. At the top was a four-sided glass lamp-shade which protected the gas mantle inside. Fixed to the fitting at the bottom of the mantle was a bracket with a chain on each side. The chains could be pulled up or down to regulate the light, in the same way as the gaslight in our kitchen. The lamp-lighter came each evening with a long pole with a hook on the end of it. He put the hook through a small ring in the end of the chain and pulled, so that the light came on. He came again in the morning and pulled the chain the opposite way, thus putting the light out. Just under the lamp-shade was an iron bar, about eighteen inches long, on which the ladder was rested when the glass was being cleaned. This iron bar afforded us a great deal of pleasure. Boys climbed the lamp-post fixing a rope, doubled over it, so that one could sit on one piece and hold on to the other. Two or three of us had a rope fixed to one lamp-post. Then we swung round the lamp-post until the rope was used up. This was great fun, even if the rope did rather cut into your bottom while swinging! Remember, we could do these things because the traffic was horse-drawn, and if we heard a horse and cart coming we could stop long before it reached us. Today, even if you were allowed to swing round lamp-posts, the traffic is so fast that it would be on you before you had a chance to get away.

Usually a ball could be obtained from someone. If there were no bats available then the ingenuity of cockney children soon became apparent. Searching in dustbins or rubbish tips until we found an old discarded milk tin, we would put it on to a long piece of wood and wait until a heavily laden van came by. Then, thrusting the can under the wheels of the van, it was quickly flattened fast to the stick. This made a fine bat and was used for cricket, tip-cat, rounders and for scraping the horse-dung off the part of the road on which we wished to play. This last was a very dangerous practice, and often re-sulted in an accident. There were no traffic wardens, no road signs, no traffic lights and plenty of carts and horses which could knock you down and trample on you should you chance to be in the way.

Cockney children were always out for a bit of fun at some-body else's expense. You could buy a packet of 'Nosegay' tobacca for twopence. The men who worked in the docks and on the river often bought a packet on their way to work. When the packet was empty it was thrown away. We had no litter bins – everything from old newspapers and tobacco packets to fish-and-chip papers, lunch papers, apple cores, orange peel and banana skins littered the streets. Boys often went hunting for old 'Nosegay' packets. Then they would pick up some dried horse-dung and fill the packet with it. This was carefully sealed up with spit and placed in a prominent position where some unsuspecting man would pick it up. Meanwhile the children were hiding in a doorway or alley. Great was their glee when the man discovered he had been 'had'. I fancy I can hear today's children scoffing at such a silly game, but then – as I have told you – we were quite content to play these games. Never having any toys worth mentioning, we were happy to improvise. Of course, there *were* toys, as I expect you have read, but these were not for us.

I remember that somewhere in Clerkenwell there was a large toy shop. I discovered it one day with Kathleen. In the window was the most wonderful doll's pram and in it sat a beautiful doll. We looked at them, spellbound. We knew we could never have them so we pretended the pram was mine and the doll belonged to Kathleen. Oh! the games we played in our imagination. Each chance we had we walked to that shop just to stand and look. Never have two children played a stranger game – with a doll and pram that they could never handle or have. Alas, we went one day and the window had been changed. The doll and the pram were gone. We cried all the way home, mourning for toys we had never possessed.

We children of the East End were always on the look-out for something for nothing. Three large wholesale markets were earmarked by us. The first was Spitalfields fruit and vegetable market. Here retailers came to buy the produce to sell in their shops. If we were patient enough to wait until the market finished, we could pick up a nice little haul from beneath the stalls. We hunted through the garbage until we were rewarded, perhaps with a few potatoes or maybe some rotting oranges and apples not good enough to sell but good enough for us if we cut away the bad. Then, if we searched hard enough, maybe we would find a yellowing cabbage, a carrot or a turnip. All these were carefully carried home to be shared and enjoyed by all.

Then there was Smithfields meat market quite near the City. Here we might find enough scraps of meat to take home for the cat. That was about all we found there, but we felt it was well worth going, if only to find enough to give the cat a free meal.

We often went to Leadenhall Market as well. This, too, was near the City. All kinds of things were sold there. We always looked around, hoping to find something that was free. We never did.

If the girls didn't feel like going to the markets, another quieter activity in which they indulged was 'A Pin for a Picture'. Pins were plentiful, because so many articles were sold at $1s\ 11\frac{3}{4}d$ or $1s\ 0\frac{3}{4}d$ which meant that you were owed $\frac{1}{4}d$ change. I mentioned earlier that it was the practice of most shops to give you a packet of pins in lieu of the farthing. Pins were used a lot to keep girls' dresses together at the back, for even if they started off with buttons these usually broke when passed through the wooden rollers of the mangle on wash-day. The girls collected old papers, old picture-books, advertisements, in fact anything that contained a picture worth having. These were carefully cut out and inserted in a large, old reading book, so that between most of the pages there was a picture of some kind. It made the book very heavy. Carrying it they would tour the streets and alleyways, calling, 'A pin for a picture, and a jolly good picture.' Children would run indoors to collect their pins. Then the book was offered to them. They closed their eyes and pushed the pin between two pages. Whatever picture they picked was theirs in exchange for the pin.

CHAPTER TWENTY-EIGHT

HAPPY EVENINGS

You may wonder how we spent our leisure time in the evenings. In the summer we played in the streets until bedtime, but in winter, when it was already dark when we came home from school, we had much to occupy us. My mother made rag mats. Any article of clothing not fit to be worn would be used. The base of the mat was a large hessian sack. We children sat on the floor each with a basin beside us. In these were placed the different coloured pieces of cloth. We cut the cloth into strips about four inches long and an inch wide. Using a sack needle, Mother would push the pieces through the hessian, leaving the two ends from each piece showing on the same side. Choosing different colours she worked until she had formed a pattern around the edge and in the centre. As the mat progressed it became very heavy and then Mother sat on the floor to work. When it was finally finished it was neatly bound on the underneath edges.

These mats were used as kitchen hearth-rugs. Needless to say, after a few weeks' wear they became full of dust and caused clouds of dirt everywhere when they were taken outside to be shaken. There were no vacuum cleaners in those days and rag mats seem now to be a thing of the past. They were so heavy that it took quite an effort to carry them. Most people who possessed one would take the easy way out and turn them face downwards indoors. Then the children would jump on them, causing the dust to go on to the floor.

When we weren't making a rag mat, we worked on patchwork quilts. Every piece of gaily coloured material was carefully saved for these, and cut into squares or shapes determined by the size of the material: sometimes they would be only two or three inches square, but every piece was used. The pieces were sewn together until a strip was made which was long enough to go over a bed, plus about a foot over. When all the strips were complete, they were joined together until the quilt was wide enough to cover a double or single bed. Once this had been done, the whole of the stitching was covered with feather-stitching to make it look pretty. Mother then lined the quilt with whatever she had to hand. If she had nothing, then we made a second patchwork and joined the two back-to-back so that the quilt could be used either side and still look nice. The quilts took many weeks to make, and sometimes only one would be made during an entire winter.

Sometimes during the dark evenings my mother would bring out a pile of darning and show us how to darn. There were flannel shirts, jerseys, socks and stockings – all with holes so large that it looked impossible that we should ever mend them. If a jersey sleeve had a great hole in it, Mother would first place a piece of an old jersey over the hole and tack in on. Then we darned over the patch and the edges of the jersey. In this way a strong darn was made which sometimes lasted after the rest of the jersey was worn out.

Stockings were darned until the feet we no longer darnable. Then the feet were cut off and the leg sewn up. This, of course, made the stocking short but then the good part of another old stocking would be joined to the top to make it long enough again. The stocking was shapeless, but as we all wore boots this did not show and the join at the top was covered by the long dresses we wore at that time.

If there was no sewing or darning to be done, we would play tunes on a large musical box. The music came from parchment rolls, when we wound the large handle on the box. We also had a Jew's harp, a small instrument which you played by placing it near the mouth and making it vibrate as you hummed a tune and knocked the side with your thumb. We had great fun with this. The noise was very unmusical, but we enjoyed it. We had a mouth-organ too, and Kathleen, William, Robert and Sydney would sing while I played it. We called all these our 'musical evenings', simple homely pleasures that I look back on as some of the happiest ones.

CHAPTER TWENTY-NINE

AN UNEXPECTED HOLIDAY

Many upper class people at the time I write about turned to Communism and Socialism, believing everything should be all for each and each for all. They came to the East End and were appalled by the conditions which existed. Some decided to take children into their homes to give them a change.

I remember one evening when my parents were out and we children were left at home. During that evening a knock came at the door. On opening it we saw a smart lady and gentleman standing there. They asked for our parents and when told they were out invited themselves in and took stock of all five of us. Looking at Kathleen, who was younger and quieter than I, they said they had come to take her for a holiday. She was to stay at Willesden, then a select suburb of London. Kathleen refused to go, but I, never at a loss, offered to go instead. My eldest brother, Robert, packed my few clothes and off I went, not knowing where I was going. My parents, on returning, were most put out at the thought of someone entering the house and taking one of us away.

As soon as we arrived at the house in Willesden I was given the first real bath I had ever had. They actually had a bathroom, and I had my own face-flannel and towel. (At home we all shared one face-flannel and one towel.) My hair was inspected to see if I was clean and then I was given supper and put to bed. The bed was wonderful, with clean white sheets and pillow-cases, two warm blankets and an eiderdown. I thought I was in heaven. At home we had sheets of a kind and one blanket (flannelette); we then put our overcoats on the top of them for warmth.

The next day was Sunday. I was given a cooked breakfast and taken to a hall for what I presumed was Sunday School. It was, but not the kind I was used to. The children were asked to go on to the platform and sing or recite. Not wanting to be left out, I offered to sing. My offer was accepted and I sang 'Gentle Jesus meek and mild, look upon a little child'. Before I could get any further, half-a-dozen hands pulled me off the platform. I was told I mustn't sing such songs. It turned out to be a Communist Sunday School, where religion was not taught, and for the short while I stayed at the house I was not allowed to go again.

CHAPTER THIRTY

PEARLY KINGS AND QUEENS

The May Day parade of decorated horses and carts was the
highlight of the month. Carmen would brush their horses until
their coats shone. Their manes and tails were washed, combed
and plaited the day before, and on the day were loosed, crimped
and shining, and tied with red-white-and-blue ribbon. Rosettes
were fixed to the bridles. The leather harness was polished.
The brass medallions shone. Even the horses's hoofs were
cleaned and polished. Altogether this was a magnificent sight.
Even the carmen's whips were decorated with ribbon and
rosettes. After work was finished for the day, the parade assembled and, I believe, made its way to Hyde Park. To me as
a child, the carts, the horses and the colours were the most
wonderful sight on earth.

In this parade walked the Pearly Kings and Queens from
nearly every borough in the East End. Thousands of pearl
buttons were sewn on to their caps, suits, dresses and hats.
The Queen's hat was a large and splendid creation. It was
covered with pearl buttons and had two large, curled ostrich
feathers on it. Not a space was left. It must have taken hours of
sewing to put on so many buttons, and the weight of the garment must have been tremendous. These Kings and Queens
were, I believe, elected by members of their particular borough.
Those who had children dressed them as Pearly Princesses
and Princes. They collected along the route for charity and
were well known for the help they gave to various institutions.
The majority were cockneys, frowned on by many perhaps;
but nowhere in the world will you find people with hearts as big
as theirs!

Summer in those far-off years was full of days when the sun

shone. The days were hot, but the nights were even hotter, for the area was so densely built up, the streets so narrow and the houses so small that the heat seemed to come and stay, making the whole area feel airless. Then people would bring chairs out and sit in the streets, leaving all doors and windows open in an attempt to cool their houses. During the working hours, the carmen put large straw-hats on the horses' heads, to protect them from the heat. The hats had holes in for the ears to go through. It was a common sight to see these, for the men had a great love for each particular horse and took as much care of it as a woman with her child.

CHAPTER THIRTY-ONE

SAVING FOR CHRISTMAS

It was the aim of every family, whatever their circumstances, to provide for a good Christmas dinner. In January of each year, the Goose Club started. This was often held in a room in a pub, or in a side room of a church hall, or club. Each Saturday evening throughout the year people paid in their contribution. A day or two before Christmas the Club shared out, and on that day each member attended and collected a large goose and a parcel of groceries. (At the time I write of geese were the accepted meal for Christmas Day.)

As I grew older these clubs closed, and loan clubs took their place. These were always held in the side room of a pub. You paid into the club so much a week. During the year you could have a loan out, paying it back with a very high interest rate. The club shared out at the end of the year. If you had had no loan during the year, your share was bigger, although it helped the club to pay a larger share-out if you *did* have a loan, for all the interest was added, after expenses had been paid, to the eventual share-out.

Many slate clubs started as well. If you joined one of these, each week you paid in the sum of one shilling a share. Then, if you were sick and off work, you could draw a few shillings a week for six weeks, plus a share-out at Christmas if the sickness benefit had not been too high. These clubs were much abused by malingerers, who often drew out more than they paid in, besides sharing the same amount at Christmas as those who had put in no claims for sickness.

All these clubs eventually closed down, as had the Goose Club. People had come to regard them as stand-bys for Christmas, but when they closed they had to manage as best they could.

There were one or two charities which helped out at Christmas time. One I remember we called 'Turner's Gift'. Under this gift, just before Christmas a hundredweight of coal would be delivered, free, to deserving people. With it came a ticket which entitled them to a free loaf of bread. This gift had been left in a bequest by one John Turner, and was administered by a church in the district.

Another good soul I remember was a seamstress. If a child, especially a boy, wore out his knickers and had nothing else to wear, she would take an old coat to pieces, turn the material and overnight make up a little suit or a pair of knickers, complete with lining. The knickers had no fly, but a small hole served the same purpose – and at least the little one was tidy and warm.

I hope you may now have some idea of the vast difference in our way of living. I write mostly for the younger generation, feeling they will understand the bewilderment some of us elderly people feel when we see and hear the things that happen today, for I feel the young can adapt so much more easily than we of the older generation. Remember, this was yesterday's world, a world seemingly far removed from today, a world of people who were just as you are but without opportunities or knowledge.

CHAPTER THIRTY-TWO

BOYS AND BEGGARS

The river was a never-ending source of pleasure. To paddle or swim in the Thames was something that every boy did. Boys would organise races between themselves. Rival gangs would compete. Each gang had its chief, a boy selected solely on merit. They would swim from one foreshore to another and back, which was usually quite a long way. Those who gave up were looked upon with contempt, while the boy that won was chosen chief of all the gangs. The boys had no lessons in swimming; they taught themselves.

The boys of working-class parents were usually tough and strong. They roughed it from a very early age. They were experts at saving lives, although their method was all their own. They were as much at home in the river as they were on land. When the ships and barges moored along the wharves on a summer's evening, swarms of boys would strip, swim out and clamber aboard, not for the purpose of stealing but for the sheer joy of it. If the vessels were moored near a river-side pub which overlooked the river, the boys would give a display of diving. Shouting to the customers to watch, they dived from the barges and ships, doing all kinds of tricks. The customers threw pennies which the boys must dive for. This afforded men and boys alike much amusement. Sometimes it ended in tragedy for, although the boys could swim, if they ventured too near a barge they were sucked under and drowned. Each boy kept a sharp look-out for anyone in trouble and many boys saved the lives of their companions while engaged in this sport.

When a boy left school at the age of fourteen there was no one to help him find a job. If he was lucky enough to be small, he might be able to get a job as page-boy in an hotel 'up West'.

Those who did this were greatly envied by the other boys. The hotel-keepers liked the boys to be as small as possible. They provided them with a smart uniform complete with brass or silver buttons. The boys lived in, and as they grew taller and older were transferred to the better paid post of doorman. Coming from homes where conditions were bad and food was poor, these boys appreciated their luck as no one else could have done! Other boys, if they had a good 'character' from their school, stood the chance of getting a job as a pan-boy, employed by the City of London Corporation. They were provided with a black, peaked cap and a white coat, and given a brush and pan. Their job was to keep the streets clear of horse-dung. There was a great deal of horse-drawn traffic on the roads: cabs, horse-drawn buses, carts, brewers' drays and hosts of other vehicles. The boys had to dodge between them to sweep up the dung. Special containers were placed at intervals on the edge of the pavement and the dung was emptied into these from the pans. Men were engaged as foremen to watch the boys and to see that each kept his allotted streets clean. The job of pan-boy was one much sought after, and it was the height of ambition of most boys to be a foreman or to be the driver of one of the carts that came to empty the containers. I wonder if the poorest in today's society would even consider such a job? The streets in the East End were not given this preferential treatment, but the City streets were required to be kept clean of dung at all times.

When World War One ended and the soldiers returned, many men found themselves unable to get work. They had served their King and country only to come home to poverty and unemployment. It was common to see bands of about six men begging. Each had a musical instrument of some kind and usually one carried a large drum. They walked along the gutters, playing and generally making a great deal of noise. One man did not play, but held a cap. And as the crowds gathered to listen and watch he went round collecting. At the end of the day each man took his share of the money and went home. It was truly a degrading way to have to live, when only a few months before they had been hailed as heroes.

I remember a certain Scotsman who came begging, clothed in full Highland dress and complete with bagpipes. He toured most of the pubs in our district and did the sword-dance while he played the bagpipes. Placing the swords on the pavement, he gave a great display of music and dancing.

There were also numerous pavement artists, who sat in prominent places to display their pictures. I particularly remember one legless man who sat outside the gates of the Tower of London. He used the paving stones as his canvas. He cleaned about eight paving stones and drew on them in coloured chalks. They were beautifully drawn pictures of flowers, country scenes and people; usually there was one of the King and Queen. The Tower attracted many visitors and many of them stood and marvelled at this man's skill. He collected quite a few coppers in two caps, one placed at each end of his drawings. He sat on a sack all day long and in the evening someone came and carried him away.

CHAPTER THIRTY-THREE

PROFITABLE PASTIMES

As Robert, my elder brother, grew older he, like the rest of the boys, wanted to make a little spending money, for none of us received any pocket money. I do not think we ever thought of asking for any. Robert somehow came into possession of a magic lantern and some glass slides. A candle was lit inside the lantern, a sheet hung up on the wall and the window was covered with some material to make the room dark. Then as each slide was pushed into a slot in the lantern, the painted picture on it was reflected on to the sheet on the wall. Robert decided to earn himself some spending money. After getting

Mother's permission, he went to his friends and offered them a magic lantern show in our bedroom at a halfpenny a show. Only boys were allowed in. They swarmed in to see the show. As the bedroom was small and the boys had to sit on the bed, only six were allowed in at a time. We members of the family were allowed in free, and we stayed for every show (which was always the same) and had great fun laughing at Robert when he put the slides in upside down or made a mistake in his running commentary of stories he invented about the slides he was showing. When the first six boys had seen the show then another six came in, and so on. Robert was certainly pleased with his takings, but he could not replace the slides with new ones and interest dwindled, for the boys, having seen the show once, did not come again.

There was another boy who was as inventive as Robert. He hired out scooters to children. Scooters had only recently been introduced and this boy had obtained a second-hand one. He decided to loan it to his friends at the rate of twopence an hour. The idea caught on, and in no time at all one could see children riding about on scooters and having the time of their lives. The boy did a roaring trade hiring them out. I longed for a ride on one, but we were strictly forbidden them. It was pointed out to us that to ride on them you had to keep one foot on the scooter and push yourself along with the other, that this would make one boot wear out very quickly and that boots were not easy to come by.

Mineral water was sold in bottles which had a glass marble fixed in the neck. You had to push the marble down before the drink would come out. Shop-keepers had a special gadget which they used to loosen the marbles. Once pushed down, the marble stayed in the neck of the bottle, tantalizingly unavailable until the bottle was smashed. As children we longed for those marbles, for they were splendid for playing with in the gutter. There was a game of chance you could play with them. If you won, you took the other person's marbles; but if you lost, then you had to wait to play again until you could collect more marbles from bottles or swap some other possession to get a few.

Another favourite pastime for boys was collecting cigarette cards. They were given in packets of certain brands of cigarettes. A game was played in the streets with these. The boys first selected a wall and a patch of pavement. Then, taking turns, each boy would press one of his cards against the wall and let it fall on the pavement. When each had let his card fall, he whose card had fallen farthest from the wall collected his own and the cigarette cards of all the other boys. Cigarette cards were highly thought of by the boys, and some who knew just how to place the cards on the wall so that they fell a long way out won all the cards from those not so skilled in the game. Old cigarette cards are collector's pieces now. I expect there is many an old man who regrets he did not keep the cards he played with as a boy.

CHAPTER THIRTY-FOUR

BABIES AND THEIR TREATMENT

As I remember my mother and her many babies, I am surprised that she ever reared any of us. Most of the babies she had were poor, delicate creatures who should never have been born. One was so frail that Mother was afraid to carry him in her arms. She would have a pillow on which to lay the baby and to carry him around. The child was two years old before he could walk, and during his short life I never saw him smile. It must have been sad, indeed, to carry a baby for nine weary months, only to find when it was born that you stood no chance of keeping it for more than a little while. This baby died just after his second birthday, but it was quite an achievement for my mother to have reared him to that age. Many babies died within a few weeks of birth.

After her first baby Mother was told that she must not have

any more. That was easier said than done, for there was nothing to prevent more babies arriving. And so they came at yearly intervals. I cannot remember ever going out to play without having a baby or younger brother or sister to mind. Needless to say, single children were few and far between.

Babies were taken out in all sorts of vehicles: homemade carts in which the baby was subject to all kinds of rough treatment; and bassinets, which had a seat at each end and a well in the middle to accommodate small feet. When the babies were too small to sit up in a bassinet, the well was covered with a board to enable the baby to lie down in some measure of comfort. Bassinets had a handle at each end and were very cumbersome and heavy. Wooden push-chairs were used for quite small babies who could not yet sit up; they had to be propped up with pillows. The poor baby was for ever sliding down and must have been most uncomfortable. All the babies, I remember, always had coughs and running noses and were regularly dosed with 'Galloways' cough mixture and rubbed with camphorated oil.

There were many mentally defective children living amongst us. These received no schooling at all when I was very young. Later, I remember, centres were opened and such children were sent there once or twice a week. Some of them were idiots quite incapable of learning anything. These poor children were not objects of pity; the rest of us took delight in tormenting and harassing them, calling after them and generally making life harder for them than it already was. In some cases, when these children grew up their parents allowed them to marry; thus the generations that followed were sometimes subnormal and in some cases cripples and idiots. Their parents were not educated in the art of bringing up subnormal children, and often they cruelly beat them because they were dirty in their habits and could not learn as other children did. Many quickly ended up in what was known as 'The Loony House' and stayed there for the rest of their lives. They were not protected by their parents, as is the case today, but sent out to play in the streets with all the other children.

Much of the suffering of the people in London's East End when I was young was unneccessary by today's standards and mainly caused by ignorance and a lack of education. It was only natural, with so many children to care for, that parents should frequently leave quite small babies in the charge of elder brothers and sisters. The parents of one family I knew once went out leaving their small baby, only a few months old, in the charge of their four elder children, whose ages ranged from five to ten years. The children rocked the pram, they shook it, they climbed on it, they took turns to see who could tip the pram up farthest without the baby falling out. The baby was not strapped in, and when eventually the pram overturned, she was pinned underneath it. The parents returned but the children, perhaps through fear of a hiding, never told them what had happened.

When the child was about two years old, her mother noticed that each time she was washing her and tried to turn her head she cried. Medical advice was sought and it was discovered that the child had a spinal injury due, it was thought, to her having been dropped when she was younger. For the whole of her childhood the little girl lay encased in a spinal jacket and was wheeled about in a spinal carriage. Eventually she was sent to St Mary's Hospital for children at Carshalton, where she remained until she was eighteen. Finally she returned home and was a hunchback for the rest of her life. We all knew her as 'Little Edie', for she never grew taller than a five-year-old. Whenever she went out with other girls, she would walk on the path while her friends walked in the road. This made her feel taller. She wore the tallest of hats and the highest of heels in an effort to make herself look taller. I think she must have suffered much mental misery, for she was bitter and jealous of her brothers and sisters all through her life. All this came about because of neglect and ignorance and the children's fear of telling their parents what had happened when they were left in charge of the baby.

The same family lost a son in the most tragic circumstances. He was five years old at the time. He was coming home from school one day when he and his companions saw a van parked, without a horse, outside a warehouse. They decided to play on the van, tethering themselves to the shafts in a pretence of being the horse. They pulled and pushed the van in an effort to get it going, until it started to move. When it started moving, it went so quickly the small boy had no chance to get away from the wall he was standing by. The van went crashing into the wall and crushed the boy. He was dead on arrival at the hospital. On another occasion, a little girl of eight years complained of a pain in her side. She was given a dose of castor oil, which in those days was a cure for all ills. During the night she gradually got worse and by the following morning she was dead. She had died from acute peritonitis.

It is a small wonder that so many people took to drink; in many cases they had a real need to drown their sorrows.

CHAPTER THIRTY-FIVE

LINSEED TEA AND TOBACCO PRICKS

During the winter almost every child developed a cough. Mother described mine as a 'graveyard' cough but, to tell the truth, I could cough to order, making it sound loud and deep. I had learned to do this with my throat, for I knew that if I coughed I would be given a dose of her home-made linseed tea. It was made from linseed, doctor's spanish (hard sticks of licorice), lemon juice and brown sugar, all boiled together until the linseed was tender and the doctor's spanish had dissolved. It was then strained into quart bottles. Throughout my childhood there was always a bottle standing on top of the kitchen cupboard, ready to dose us with. We loved taking it, for it was very pleasant to the taste and a cheap and easy way of dosing children.

Something the men used to like and which helped them to concentrate was chewing a slice cut from a prick of tobacco. It was mostly a habit of lightermen and watermen. Taking a piece of tobacco leaf they would roll it very tightly, then wind it round with yarn which had been treated with Stockholm Tar. Over this went more tobacco leaf, then more yarn, until it was about three-quarters of an inch thick and about eight inches long. It would then be soaked in rum and left to harden. When hard, it was impossible to break. When a piece was needed for chewing, the men would take a sharp knife and cut a slice off. This lasted a long time, the men getting the flavour of the tobacco and rum.

The pubs catered only for the dockers and river workers. They provided spittoons placed at intervals around the floor. These were for spitting the used pricks of tobacco into. The floor was liberally sprinkled with sawdust for the men were not particular as to what was spat out onto it. These homemade pricks of tobacco were a substitute for the real thing, for men would have chewed tobacco had it been obtainable. Very often the men made pricks of tobacco, then went to another pub where they were not known, and sold them for the real thing, getting as much as fifteen or twenty shillings for one prick. This was quite a large amount and it gave the men a nice little profit, as well as a laugh for being clever enough to pass off the substitute for the real thing to the unsuspecting buyers.

CHAPTER THIRTY-SIX

EVICTION AND GRANDAD NEXT DOOR

Nowadays an eviction makes national news, but it was not so when I was young. Rents were often only a few shillings a week, but wages were low and even the few shillings charged was more than some people could manage to pay. When the rent man called, people who owed rent were too afraid to open their doors. Most property was owned by private landlords, and as far as I can remember there were no council houses. Most landlords were wealthy people. We never saw them and I doubt very much if they ever visited their properties, or if they even knew precisely where they were. If the rents were not paid for a few weeks, then you were evicted.

We knew one family of ten (father, mother and eight children) who lived in a tenement. Like ours, it consisted of two bedrooms and a kitchen. The children were noisy and quarrelsome and the father spent most of his time in the pub, but the mother was a clean, hardworking woman, who tried desperately hard to make ends meet. She fell behind with the rent and was served with an eviction order. The parents searched desperately for another place to live but could find nothing. Finally they went out for the whole day to search for a place, leaving the children at home. While they were out the eviction order was carried out. The children and the entire contents of the home were all dumped into the street and the tenement was locked up. In the evening the parents returned, having found an even smaller tenement in which to live. It was with great distress that they saw what had happened. Together mother, father and children carried their bits and pieces to the new home. They were lucky, for at least they had found somewhere else to live. Had they not they would have ended up, like so many others, in the workhouse.

A family came to live next door to us, from King's Lynn in Norfolk. They were father, mother, four girls and a grandfather. They had two bedrooms, as we did. The father was a horse-keeper for a firm of cartage contractors. For work he wore heavy breeches, leather gaiters and heavy leather boots. He was charming to talk to and polite and courteous to all he met, but nobody liked him. Many of the boys in the district helped the carmen with the horses. These men and boys treated the horses very well, having a great regard for their welfare. This man was in charge of the horses during weekends and any other time they were in the stables. His job was to feed and water the horses, clean out the stalls and give each horse clean straw to lie on. Somehow the horses sensed that this man was cruel, for they were always restive and uneasy when he was about. Word got around that he thrashed the horses, which of course made him everyone's enemy. Added to this was his wife's treatment of the grandfather. When she went out she would turn him out of the house. This happened in all weathers, even during the winter. If it was not raining or snowing he would go for a walk, but if it was too bad he would stand in the shelter of the tenement passage, stamping his feet and trying to keep warm. In fine weather he went for a walk, but being old and slow this soon tired him. He would come back and patiently wait until he was let into the house again. He always looked cold, miserable and unhappy.

By a coincidence our front door key fitted theirs and one day my mother feeling sorry for the old man, let him in with our key. This was not regarded as a kindness by his daughter-in-law, who came and told Mother not to let him in again. The next time he stood waiting in the cold, Mother asked him into our home. She gave him a cup of tea, and let him warm himself. He was so grateful and such a gentle old man that we children all wished he was our grandfather. His gratitude to my mother was most touching. Alas this small kindness was not to last. My mother was told not to have him in the house, and so poor grandfather had to stay out.

He was never allowed to eat or sit with his family. His meals were given to him, and while he ate them he had to sit apart from the family. He was treated as an outcast. We all felt very strongly about this, but there was nothing we could do except be nice to him when we saw him. He never spoke of the way he was treated, but I was friendly with one of the girls and often went there and saw for myself what the family's treatment of him was. He died during one very cold winter. Everyone, without exception, felt that his daughter-in-law was indirectly responsible for his death. She had been a strong, big, buxom woman when they first came to live next door and one could, as the saying is, 'have taken a lease on her life'. But one day, soon after the grandfather had died, she was doing her normal work, when she was taken ill. The doctor was called and said that she must stay in bed. About a fortnight later I went in to see her. I was shocked at the change. During that short time she had fallen away and was but a ghost of her former self. Soon afterwards, she died from cancer. People in those days were very superstitious and it was the general opinion that 'God had paid a debt without money'.

CHAPTER THIRTY-SEVEN

'UNCLE' AND OLD LADIES

You must have realised by now how different life was in the times and community in which I lived. Then there was a pride in overcoming difficulties. Hard times came to everyone; to fight each trouble as it came along was the order of the day. Of course there were the exceptions, and those who would not or could not help themselves were helped as far as possible by neighbours, not with money but in kind.

I remember each Monday morning seeing a certain woman going from door to door collecting little bundles. She would take them to the pawn-shop and pawn them for a shilling or two, and then come back again, giving out the money to those for whom she had taken them. I would see her go again on Friday and return with the goods she had redeemed from the pawn-shop. To pawn your valuables was better than asking your neighbours for help, which they most probably could not have given. The valuables weren't really needed, and we laughed the matter off by saying, 'Uncle (the pawn-shop man) might as well mind them for us.'

My mind also goes back to certain homeless women who

lived in the East End in the Salvation Army hostel. They each had a bed, for which I believe they paid sixpence a night, but they had to go out during the daytime and were not allowed in again until the evening. They wandered about the streets during the day, carrying their few possessions with them, trying to find a job that would earn them the sixpence with which to pay for their bed.

When Reuben and I were first married we lived in two rooms on the top floor of an old house, as I have told you. The rest of the house was occupied as a tailor's workshop and home by the tailor and his large family. I often saw the tailor's wife standing at her door waiting for one of these homeless women to come by. When she saw a likely one, she would offer her sixpence and her dinner if she did a day's work for her. I never saw any woman refuse her offer. She did the whole of the weekly wash for eight people, cleaned the house and was kept fully occupied for most of the day. At the end of it she collected her sixpence, knowing that she could pay for her bed that night and hopeful of finding another job the next day.

CHAPTER THIRTY-EIGHT

MILE END WASTE

I do not know where my parents obtained the beds we children slept in. I only know they were old-fashioned, wire-sprung beds fixed on to a wooden frame. Three children slept in one bed and two in the other. These beds were uncomfortable and dirty. The springs were broken, so that the flock mattress could not lay flat on it. Consequently, when laid upon, it was, as we laughingly said, 'up hill and down dale'.

One year, as Guy Fawkes approached, Father decided that we would have a bonfire in the drying-yard behind the tenements. This was not, as you might think, in order to give us a treat but to burn our beds. We had all caught scarlet fever that year, and Mother was quite convinced that the beds had had something to do with it. Kathleen was the first to contract it. She was taken to the isolation hospital, where she stayed for six weeks, but this proved to be no deterrent and when she returned my brothers and I all contracted it in turn, at six-weekly intervals. As soon as one came home from the isolation hospital another caught it. Mother thought that she had caught it too, and certainly she had the same symptoms but she refused to get attention for fear of being sent away, and thus having to leave the family to fend for themselves. So she nursed herself back to a fair state of health.

Whether her suspicions were correct or not I do not know, but Father took all the beds into the yard on Guy Fawkes Night and burned them as part of the largest bonfire I had ever seen. Then we went to the Mile End Waste, borrowed a barrow and bought three second-hand hospital beds, of black iron and complete with mattresses. The Mile End Waste, by the way, was a place off the Whitechapel Road where the flotsam and jetsam that no one wanted any longer was sold. You could buy almost anything there: clothing, boots, bicycles, tools, pictures and furniture of every description, all displayed on the ground or stacked on barrows. During the week, fruit and vegetable barrows lined the road but on Saturdays it was crowded with everything imaginable.

Father wheeled the beds back home. Kathleen and I had to share one, William and Sydney another, while Robert (being the eldest) had the third to himself. Throughout the rest of my childhood, and in fact until I married, I had to share a bed with Kathleen. As we grew older it became very cramped indeed, and if either of us wanted to turn over or shift our position we had to do so together. I always envied Robert having a bed to himself, but sharing had its compensation; Kathleen and I were always sure of being warm, even on the bitterest winter's night.

CHAPTER THIRTY-NINE

FATHER AND HIS MOTHER

I would not say my father was a religious man, yet he had a high set of standards which he imposed on us children. I never ever heard him swear, and I never knew him lose his temper. He was stern and unloving, and yet he was a good father compared to many at the time. He had no friends, but didn't seem worried by this, I feel he was a little contemptuous of the men with whom he worked. He held himself aloof and never mixed. This attitude made him disliked by everyone. He condemned drinking, high heels, make-up and dancing.

Thinking of him now, I believe he was influenced greatly by his mother. She had had a large family and kept them all strictly under her thumb. When he was courting my mother, his family lived on old London Bridge, which was an hour's walk away from where my mother lived. One evening they went to a concert. He saw my mother home and it was ten-thirty before he reached his house. He found he was locked out. When he knocked at the door his mother put her head out of the upstairs window and told him to go back where he had been. So that night he walked the streets. I can remember his mother visiting us once. My mother prepared a dinner so that she could share it with us, but when she came she brought with her a piece of black pudding. She refused our dinner, saying she preferred her own. As we children came in we were all reprimanded in turn because we put our hands on the wall. She appreciated nothing my mother did; she just sat and judged us all. Needless to say, we did not love her and were glad she never came again. I have a vague memory of aunts and uncles, sisters and brothers of Father's. They all seemed to be above our station and better off than we were. I only remember them visiting us once, in order to discuss grandmother. From what I gathered from the conversation they were all most concerned and indignant because they were being asked to contribute towards her keep, now that she was in the Union's Hospital. She had been widowed and had had no means of support other than her old-age pension, which in those days was only a few shillings a week. Even this was taken away when she entered the Union.

Father had been asked to pay two shillings a week towards her keep. He refused to pay, saying he could not afford it because he had a family to support. My aunts and uncles all gave reasons why they too could not pay a few shillings a week to ensure their mother's welfare. As I mentioned, she was hard and unloving towards her grandchildren but she must surely at some time in her life have loved her children, must have tended and cared for them, must have made sacrifices for them. Yet there they were, meeting for the first time in my father's house to agree on one course of action. They decided to stick together and refuse to pay anything at all. I'm sure that my proud and loveless grandmother, had she heard the arguments which filled our home that day, would, like me, have gone away and silently wept.

I visted her in the Union and she welcomed me. She said no one ever went to see her and she asked me to go again. I went several times before she died. Father knew I went to see her but never once did he ask how she was or offer to come with me. It is sad indeed not to be loved or not to have the ability to love, for to love and be loved is sheer happiness.

CHAPTER FORTY

A VISIT TO THE CINEMA

One particular event stands out in my mind. It was a Sunday afternoon and I tried to persuade Kathleen to come with me to the Premierland Cinema in Backchurch Lane. She pointed out that it was a Sunday and that it was wicked to go to the pictures on Sunday. Wicked or not, I was not in the least worried by that. What did worry me was the possibility of my parents finding out. Eventually, after much argument, I had my way and we went. The entrance fee was twopence each. Where we obtained our money I cannot remember, but we had it and I was all set to enjoy the afternoon.

It was a silent film called 'Broken Blossoms', staring Lilian Gish. I sat enthralled, transported into another world. Presently I heard a sniff. Looking at Kathleen I saw she was crying bitterly. Surprised, I asked her what was the matter. 'Oh, Grace, come out! It's wicked and God will punish us,' she cried. She made such a to-do that I very reluctantly came out in the middle of the most interesting part. I'm sorry to say I nagged poor Kathleen all the way home, for I had no conscience at all.

CHAPTER FORTY-ONE

GRASS BETWEEN THE CRACKS

I longed to put a little colour around me when I was a child. The drying yard at the back of the tenements was cobbled and looked grey and cheerless. There was a crack of earth between each stone. The horses were fed with chaff, with the result that if you searched for long enough it was possible to scrape up a little bagful. I decided one day to collect as much chaff as I was able and plant it in the yard. Each bag I collected I carefully put in earth between the cobblestones. The yard was quite large for it stretched the width of the tenements. I collected chaff for many weeks and continued to sprinkle it between the cracks. No so long after, on looking out one day, I saw a faint tinge of green, and as successive days went by the whole yard was gradually filled with the grass growing between the cracks. The satisfaction and joy I experienced when looking at my grass far outweighed any bouquet or flowers I have since been bought. The colour was there as a result of something I had thought of and grown by myself. It was a truly wonderful feeling of achievement in such a grey world.

When my mother used carrots or turnips for a meal the tops were never thrown away. She had to save them for me. Placed in an old tin lid filled with water, they afforded me endless pleasure as I watched the tiny shoots grow and the leaves form. I thought the carrot-tops were especially beautiful, with their delicate, feathery leaves. They did not last long, for I sometimes forgot to give them fresh water, but there were always more to replace them. The pleasure in watching them grow can only be appreciated by those who love colour and gardens, and are denied them.

As I write I see another blaze of colour; it is as if it were yesterday. In the Tower of London, in front of the Traitor's Gate, was a gorgeous array of marigolds. They shone like burnished gold when the sun shone on them. Traitor's Gate was one of my favourite places and I used to go just to look at the marigolds. With the grey walls of the Tower behind them they presented a feast of colour, one I never tired of looking at. I wonder if they are still there, or has progress destroyed them?

CHAPTER FORTY-TWO

WHEN ALL IS SAID AND DONE

To many it may seem that we lived a miserable existence, but I do assure you that this was not always the case. I never worried then over the conditions as I saw them. I, along with the rest of the children, was carefree, happy, noisy, cheeky and cheerful. We enjoyed life, much as I suppose children can in most circumstances. People of that era knew how to make the best of every situation. They were happy and carefree in good times and sad when days were grim, but to live and to know that you had neighbours who cared about you and on whom you could rely as friends and helpers indeed made up for the lack of money and material things; and even as I recall the poverty and the squalor which there were amid the hustle and bustle, the noise and the dirt, the narrow streets and dark alleys, I feel a great sense of nostalgia for this unlovely place, for there as well were to be found comradeship and happiness.

Now the horse and carts are gone. Children no longer play in the streets. The sounds of shipping on my part of the river are hushed now, for the great docks in that area are gone. The cobbled roads have been replaced by asphalt and tar. And wherever you look you will see even higher buildings replacing the high walls in whose shadows I spent my childhood.